Another Day in

Post-Racial America:

To the Mothers of the Black

Lives Matter Movement, With

Love

Dianne Liuzzi Hagan and Ronald Hagan, c. 1993

Another Day in Post-Racial America: To the Mothers of the Black Lives Matter Movement, With Love

Dianne Liuzzi Hagan

HaganWorkz
Winston Salem, NC

Another Day in Post-Racial America: To the Mothers of the Black Lives Matter Movement, With Love is a work of nonfiction.

Published by HaganWorkz
Haganworkz@gmail.com

Cover Photo by Ronald F. Hagan
Title Page Photo by Cara Hagan and Mackenzie Hagan
Page 111 Photo by Ronald F. Hagan

ISBN-13: 9781797509044

BISAC: Social Science / Ethnic Studies / African American Studies / General

Dedication

To the Mothers of the Black Lives Matter movement:
Sybrina Fulton
Lezley McSpadden
Gwen Carr
Geneva Reed-Veal
Cleopatra Pendleton-Cowley
Maria Hamilton
Lucy McBath
And all the mothers and fathers who lost sons or daughters
to Jim Crow and the racists who support it

And to the founders of the Black Lives Matter movement:
Alicia Garza
Opal Tometi
Patrisse Cullors
And all the individuals who continue to organize, march,
and protest peacefully against modern-day Jim Crow

Rest in Power
Amadou Diallo, LaTanya Haggerty, Kendra James, Ronald
Madison, Sean Bell, Manuel Loggins Jr., Ramarley Graham,
Shereese Francis, Rekia Boyd, Jamar Clark, Yvette Smith,
Tamir Rice, Laquan McDonald, Akai Gurley, Eric Garner,
Ezell Ford, Michael Brown Jr., Christian Taylor, Walter
Scott, Natasha McKenna, Freddie Gray, Brendon
Glenn, Dontre Hamilton, Samuel DuBose, Gregory
Gunn, Akiel Denkins, Alton Sterling, Philando Castile,
Terence Crutcher, Keith Lamont Scott, Jonny Gammage,
Jordan Edwards
Trayvon Martin, Darius Simmons, Jordan Davis, Emmett
Till, James Craig Anderson, Timothy Caughman, Richard
Collins III

Rev. Clementa Pinckney, Cynthia Hurd, The Rev. Sharonda Coleman-Singleton, Tywanza Sanders, Ethel Lance, Susie Jackson, Depayne Middleton Doctor, The Rev. Daniel Simmons, Myra Thompson, Cynthia Wesley, Carole Robertson, Addie Mae Collins, Denise McNair, Heather Heyer

And all the individuals who lost their lives at the hands of racist police officers, vigilantes, or white supremacist terrorists

No one can bring back those you've lost. No one has the capacity to heal your broken hearts or to eradicate hatred and racism from the hearts and minds of others, but each one of us has the capacity to feel sorrow for your losses and outrage for how your sons and daughters lost their lives, to pledge remembrance, to acknowledge racism is systemic, to stand with you in this struggle, to believe equality and equal treatment under the law are inherent rights, to state unequivocally that black lives matter, to hope for a better tomorrow, and to act together toward that end.

Table of Contents

Introduction
Mothers of the Movement

On October 22, 2016 my husband Ronald and I, an interracial couple, (I am white and Ronald is black), who have been together for more than forty years, were catching a late lunch at a new barbecue restaurant in downtown Winston-Salem, North Carolina. Our lunches had been served, and we were chatting and eating, when a group of women walked by our table to be seated. They came from behind me, so I did not see their faces. One made eye contact with Ronald, and they nodded at one another and said, "Hello." Ronald said, "I know her. I've seen her on TV."

"Maybe she is a local newscaster," I said.

"No," he said. "Someone from the national news."

As the hostess seated the women, I looked over and my mouth popped open. "You're right! That's Sandra Bland's mother. And there is Trayvon Martin's mother, and Eric Garner's mother."

The other women were the mothers of Jordan Davis and Dontre Hamilton, and perhaps the last woman, whom I could not identify, was assigned as a local guide. The mothers are Geneva Reed-Veal, Sybrina Fulton, Gwen Carr, Lucy McBath, and Maria Hamilton. They are members of a club of women who lost children to violence perpetrated by police officers or vigilantes. Sybrina Fulton was the first to create an alliance with the Black Lives Matter Movement, which rose out of the protests over her son Trayvon Martin's murder at the hands of neighborhood watch coordinator George Zimmerman. As the list of murdered sons and daughters grew, they formed a club no one would ever wish to join.

Perhaps one of the first mothers who openly grieved the loss of her son was Mamie Till-Mobley, mother of Emmet Till, who was murdered on August 28, 1955. He had been accused of whistling at a white woman. That woman, Carolyn Bryant, admitted, when she was in her eighties, that she lied about what occurred on the day Till went to buy a piece of gum at the store where she was the cashier. She was not charged because the statute of limitations expired long before her confession.

Mamie Till-Mobley not only openly grieved the loss of her son, she demanded the world share in her grief and horror when she allowed *Jet Magazine* and *The Chicago Defender* to publish photographs of her dead son, unrecognizable after the severe torture he endured at the hands of Carolyn Bryant's husband and her brother in the last hours of his life. He was 14 years old. The vigilantes were acquitted, but when *Look* magazine offered them $4,000, their detailed confessions were published in an article titled "The Shocking Story of Approved Killing in Mississippi." Those photographs, the published confessions, and the outrage they elicited across America fueled the Civil Rights Movement, just as Trayvon Martin's murder fueled the formation of Black Lives Matter.

I knew the mothers had come into Winston-Salem that day to rally for Hillary Clinton, but I did not feel like fighting the crowds to go to the campaign rally as I had with my daughter Cara and her husband Robert in 2008, when we drove to Charlotte to see then-Senator Barack Obama and I had, amazingly, gotten to shake his hand. What I did not expect was to see these women anywhere outside of the rally where, in this red-leaning state, they would be subject to the curious or the cruel.

Ronald and I picked at our food. The speakers blared country music, and waitresses rushed by our table to serve others. I could not say if anyone else in the restaurant knew who these women were or what burdens they carried.

"I wish I could go over and speak to them. At least offer my condolences. But I'm too emotional. Why should they have to comfort me?"

Ronald nodded in agreement. My empathy is as well known to family and friends as is his dark cynicism. Each time the news reveals another unarmed black man, woman, or child violated or murdered at the hands of a police officer, vigilante, or domestic terrorist, we both feel loss, injustice, sorrow, helplessness, and hopelessness.

I remember Rodney King and the riots sparked by the acquittal of the police officers involved in the high-speed chase and traffic stop on March 3, 1991, during which King was beaten nearly to death. Seven policemen were involved. Four were videotaped beating him with their batons while the others stood by. Many Americans did not know about police brutality, but this time it was caught on tape, played over and over on the news, and indelibly proved that if you are black in America interactions with law enforcement tend to be negative and can quickly escalate to dangerous and even fatal levels. The riots that began immediately after the acquittal of the four charged police officers on April 29, 1992 lasted six days, caused millions of dollars in damage, and led to fifty-three deaths and thousands of people injured. The National Guard was called in.

I sat sobbing in front of the TV, 3,000 miles away in Syracuse, New York. Despair oozed through me as Los Angeles burned on my twin daughters' eighth birthday. Cara and Mackenzie wanted to know why I was so sad. I told them I was crying for all the people who felt other Americans hated them, treated them differently and brutally, wished they were not part of America, and then blamed them for their poverty and disenfranchisement. The only thing they could do from their powerless status in America was to destroy whatever crossed their path. I cried because I had always been afraid the police might do something like that to Ronald, just for being black. He had many scary run-ins with the police, and sometimes, my daughters and I witnessed them.

Cara and Mackenzie also witnessed the times we were treated poorly for being an interracial couple, like when they were just two, and the estate executor of the house we were trying to buy rushed over when a neighbor alerted her that the realtor had let us in for a final walk-through. She yelled at our toddlers, as if they were adults, and demanded to know why we were there. When we told her, she laughed and said she had no idea when she would agree to a closing date. And that was after we had won the housing discrimination suit filed through the New York State Division of Human Rights, because, when she found out we were an interracial family, she refused to honor our purchase agreement. She said we'd throw chicken bones out the kitchen window, cause the house values to drop, and ruin the neighborhood, and she wouldn't do that to her sister-in-law's neighbors.

We were tired from all the months of meetings with mediators and attorneys, our apartment landlord asking us daily when we were leaving and threatening not to extend our lease another month, and family and friends telling us to drop the whole thing and find another house. We felt we had to go through with it, because we didn't want the girls to grow up thinking that people could tell them where they could or couldn't live. Besides, that was the third realtor we worked with, because the other two refused to show us houses in that neighborhood, which was just a couple of blocks from our apartment complex. One had our credit checked without our permission before he submitted an offer on another house in a black middle class neighborhood. His delay caused us to lose the house to another offer. The other one showed us hovels and told us that was all we could afford. As we left the house that day of the final walk-though, each one of us holding a child protectively, to shield them from that woman's harping threats, we both wished the whole debacle would end. She would hold out on the closing until 4:00 in the afternoon on the day our mortgage offer was to expire. Her attorney attended the closing as her proxy. Our realtor harassed us for the next year, because she never paid his commission. He sued her, and she countersued him for defamation of character. I often woke up screaming from a recurring nightmare in which the executor and her son set the house on fire and watched it burn while we were trapped inside.

Cara and Mackenzie also witnessed the time Ronald was questioned by the school resource officer for going into the school to pick them up one day, after quite a few white parents preceded him through the door without question, and when the Brownie troop leader told him, when he got to the school late to pick them up, that they were kicked out of the troop. He tried to explain he had been at a working fire and could not be relieved or take time to contact her or me, but she accused him of disliking her for being "an assertive white woman." Then she tried to hit him with her car door, right after her son gave Ronald the finger from the back seat, and Ronald called him on it. We complained to the Girl Scouts, including a meeting with the regional director, but she said they couldn't get rid of the troop leader because they couldn't find enough volunteers. Our daughters had to end their short scouting career, along with almost every other girl of color in the troop, who had also been kicked out for one infraction or another.

They felt the unfairness of such incidents. Those incidents shaped them into adults who know silence is complicity and that the world is an unfair and dangerous place, especially if your skin is brown.

The first time I witnessed a police stop was in college in the mid-1970s. We had been dating for about a year, and Ronald had borrowed his dad's car so he could take me on a date off Syracuse University's campus. Toward the end of the evening, he pulled into the parking lot of a building in downtown Syracuse, where he and his brothers rented a rehearsal studio for their band. He wanted to show me the studio and his drum kit, but, instead, we stayed in the car talking and listening to the radio, something we still do for hours, even now, decades later. Soon we saw blue lights as a cop car pulled up beside us. I was stunned. I had never been in a car that got pulled over, nor did I know the police could stop you for sitting and talking in a legally parked car.

The white cop, his hand on his gun, leaned down to the driver's side window, looked past Ronald, and, checking me over, said, "Young lady, are you in this car voluntarily?"

"Yes."

"You know this man?"

"He's my boyfriend."

"Your boyfriend," he said, and I could feel the sneer in his voice. "How old are you?"

"I'm nineteen."

Then he looked at Ronald and said, "Did you force her in this car?"

"No, I did not. I'd appreciate it if you treated my lady with respect."

"What are you doing here?"

"My band rents a studio here in the building."

"I could check on that." It registered as a threat, and I could feel my heart racing.

"Go ahead and check," Ronald said, his voice hard-edged.

"Look, why don't you just move along? I better not see you here with her again," the cop said, his bluff called.

"You might. I rehearse here, and she may come to listen," Ronald said. I learned then that Ronald would assert his right to be in public spaces no matter who tried to claim otherwise.

King famously appeared before the press and pled with the rioters to stop. He asked, "Can't we all get along?"

He became the symbol of victimization by racist police. His beating may have opened the public's eyes to police brutality, but I knew police misconduct and prejudice existed before Officers Koon, Powell, Wind, and Briseno beat King, and I know they still exist.

I remember Jonny Gammage, a man from Syracuse, the city I called home for thirty-two years, who was killed by officers on October 12, 1995 outside Pittsburgh, Pennsylvania, where his cousin, Ray Seals, played for the Steelers. He was driving Seals' Jaguar when he was pulled over. His dying words to Sergeant Keith Henderson of the Whitehall police department as he suffocated under the pressure of a cop's knee on his neck and upper torso, were, "Keith, Keith, I'm 31. I'm only 31."

Outrage and fear consumed me when the story broke. The situation felt so close to home, like the time Ronald went to unlock our Toyota Celica and felt the cold metal of a gun barrel against the back of his head. The officer told him, "Blacks don't own foreign cars." Or of the many times we were stopped and I was asked, as I was that first time in the 1970s, if I were in the car of my own volition. Or the many times he was pulled over and asked if he owned the car or motorcycle he was driving. The assumptions were always that he had stolen them or gotten them with money earned through drug dealing or some other illegal activity. Even though he bought those vehicles with the salary he earned serving our community for twenty-five years as a firefighter, just the third black officer in the history of the department, the police assumed the worst. It's called racial bias, and it is sometimes deadly.

Racial bias has no place in our country, and especially no place in our police departments. The police should be trained to assess each situation as unique. They should not go in amped up because the person they are stopping is a person of color and the officer has already imagined the worst. The worst can happen at any stop, no matter the race of the person, so racial bias in the other direction can be dangerous as well. Cops, like firefighters, sign up for danger. Their training should reflect that. Yet it often seems they forget their training and simply react based on false assumptions and stereotypes of people of color.

Ronald has often explained to me how he got through service in the fire department by saying that, no matter how scared you are, you let the training take over. You go through the steps. Otherwise, all firefighters, if they relied simply on feeling, would be running out of the fires instead of into them, or a lot more of them would die in the line of duty.

Police in our communities should be peace officers, protecting and serving all citizens. Instead, they have become a militarized presence that controls the actions of certain citizens.

Mother Jones described the militarization of police departments this way: "Welcome to a new era of American policing, where cops increasingly see themselves as soldiers occupying enemy territory, often with the help of Uncle Sam's armory, and where even nonviolent crimes are met with overwhelming force and brutality."

Police work requires dealing with people who are in crisis, and it is up to the police officer to de-escalate the situation. Many police officers are good at this, and their departments support it, departments like the Dallas police department under the leadership of now-retired Chief Ron

Brown, who once posted to Facebook, "The citizens of Dallas have shown great trust and confidence in the Dallas Police Department. My pledge is that we will continue to work as hard to maintain and improve citizens' trust as we did to earn it." They practice transparency, community policing, do not use traffic tickets as a form of revenue, reflect the racial makeup of their communities, and work hard to work with the community as partners, not adversaries.

Other officers do not have the skills required for good policing. They allow their inherent racial bias to determine whom they will stop and how they will conduct themselves during the stop. They quickly escalate a stop for a traffic infraction or for looking suspicious, which is also often related to racial bias. That kind of policing assumes every person of color walking or driving by the officer is the enemy. It causes police, like former State Trooper Brian Encinia of Waller County, Texas, to precipitate a pullover as he did on July 10, 2015. The dashcam shows Encinia's vehicle racing up to Sandra Bland's car, dangerously tailgating her, and prompting her to change lanes without signaling.

He escalates the stop, threatening to tase her if she doesn't leave the vehicle. He also takes her out of camera range, but the viewer can still hear the increasing fear in her voice as he apparently throws her to the ground. Bland, a college graduate driving to another state to begin a new position at her alma mater, mysteriously died in jail instead of starting her new career. I can only imagine how her mother, Geneva Reed-Veal, received the news of her death or, in the days following, the details of her daughter's last days on earth. It broke my heart, as each of the other publicized murders has. My mind reels when I think of all the murders that did not make national news.

Maybe Reed-Veal's loss of her daughter left me more emotional because I am the mother of twin daughters, and there had been few previous stories of women and police brutality in the news. I remember the fear I felt when we sent our daughters 700 miles away to finish high school at a dance conservatory in the South. We dropped them off just two weeks before 9/11. They were 17 and racially ambiguous, so I worried after 9/11 that someone would target them as Arabs.

That never happened, but their foray into a predominately white school was painful enough. Some kids refused to speak to them because they were black, from New York, and possibly, one student opined, carrying box cutters. Mackenzie was quick to respond, "We're middle-class kids just like you," but my daughters still felt isolated, particularly in that first year, when there were so few students of color and only one or two teachers of color on the whole campus. They came from an urban school environment with an ethnic minority student population at close to fifty percent. Ronald and I agonized over whether or not we made the right decision to send them into a mostly white place that didn't feel welcoming, but as Ronald has often said, "If I stopped going everywhere white people didn't want me to go, I'd never go anywhere."

My daughters ended up doing fine for four years at the conservatory, graduating with bachelor of fine arts degrees, and they have gone on to lead accomplished adult lives, but they often share stories of microaggressions and worse. I know it doesn't end, and, truthfully, when they were children my biggest fear was of them losing their father, because I was terrified a police stop would end his life.

Ronald's arrest was a misdemeanor for trespassing. He had met a group of guys at the neighborhood bar to talk about starting a band. They bought him two beers that evening. He is not a drinker, and on his way home, he pulled his car over and decided to walk the rest of the way. The police picked him up a couple blocks from his car. The cops said they had a report of a trespasser looking in the windows of a student apartment on a street Ronald had not walked. They claimed they followed footprints in the snow, which led to him. They told him that there were no black people living in the neighborhood, even though his parents lived less than four blocks away, and he was less than a mile from our home. The police did not believe he was a firefighter. They tried to bang his head on the doorframe when they guided him into the back of the squad car. They towed his car. They said they would make sure they inconvenienced him and cost him money, even if they couldn't make the charges stick. They would not give him his right to a phone call until after they had checked with central fire to confirm he was a firefighter. He called me at 6:00 a.m. after I had frantically spent the night calling area hospitals, looking to see if he had been brought into the emergency room. I was sure he was dead. The attorney we hired to represent him told him to be happy they hadn't beaten him before they put him in the car. He said the only thing that saved him was the off chance he had told the truth and he really was a firefighter, a brother in service. The charge was dismissed, but, indeed, it cost us money.

I worried that next time, a cop would shoot Ronald four or five times and kill him before he asked questions, leaving me a widow and our daughters without a father. Then he would be tried in the media and in public as some kind of deserving thug, while the cop would get off, as hundreds of others have. I worried about that more than I worried about him getting hurt on the job as a firefighter, one of the people who ran into the fire, not out, or who fought fires from above, two or three stories up, balanced on steep-pitched roofs covered in ice and snow, cutting ventilation holes with a chainsaw, fire just beams and shingles below him.

Ms. Reed-Veal's courage and her determination to speak to the country along with the other Mothers of the Movement made me want to tell them that even though I cannot know the depth of their loss, I do feel outrage, sorrow, and fear. Even though I have lived in an interracial relationship my entire adult life, (Ronald and I met when I was 18 and he was 19), and raised mixed-race daughters, I can never know exactly what it is to be black in America and to know the systemic oppression and the violence directed at black communities. What I do know, with my deepest emotion and conviction, is that black lives matter.

My experiences have been eye-opening and, at times, terrifying. I have felt the power of contempt, hatred, and bias, so I know, even though I am imbued with privilege by virtue of my skin color, that racism exists, is systemic and institutional, and impacts Americans of color socially, economically, and sometimes fatally.

In the 1990s I started documenting my experiences. After Jonny Gammage was killed, I wrote a short article titled "Am I Safe?" that was published in *Interrace Magazine,* and later in the Greenhaven Press Current Controversies Anthology *Police Brutality.* I wanted others to know what we experienced, because often, the telling of our stories was met with disbelief. Just as President Obama was being sworn into office in 2009, I started my second master's degree in creative nonfiction writing. I wanted to get better at telling our stories.

After graduating with my MFA in December 2010, I started a blog called *About Race.* I post about race, culture, gender, politics, and ethnicity, through my personal experience—a serial memoir. The arc of my storytelling matched the arc of Obama's rise to power and the attendant declarations of post-racialism contrasted with threats and claims he was an illegitimate leader. I always knew those who asserted we were now living in a post-racial society were simply naïve, in denial, or indifferent.

All one had to do was to hear and watch President Obama being attacked at unprecedented levels. Many of the charges against him, using the coded words of racism, claimed he was un-American. It echoed the way in which many of the victims of police brutality were quickly assassinated a second time as the media painted them as thugs deserving of brutality and death.

As the number of fatalities at the hands of the police and vigilantes grew along with reported incidents of calling the police on black Americans for such imagined violations as napping in the dorm lounge, wearing socks in the pool area, grilling in a public park, or paving a parking lot, I also began using the line "Just another day in post-racial America" to post these stories to my Facebook pages. I wanted my friends and readers to know these incidents were commonplace and that America had not reached a post-racial state and was not even close. Rather, things were as they have been for hundreds of years, where racism is systematized and institutional, racial bias is widely accepted in the mainstream, and, as has been noted in history time and again, backlashes against racial progress were mounting.

We experienced it in our lives, too, in microaggressions and worse. Like the times Ronald is questioned for being by my side, like at the deli counter in the grocery store, week after week, where we are standing together next to a grocery cart, chatting while our order is filled, and Ronald is asked if he needs something or told he will be helped in a few minutes, because the deli worker cannot fathom we are together and is concerned this black man is standing too close to a white woman, or someone thinks he is bothering me while we wait in line at the movie theater or walk through a store. Just another day in our interracial marriage.

We heard similar stories from others. Once the cable guy told me that every time he had a service call in one particular neighborhood, the police were alerted to a suspicious person. Apparently he was a crafty robber with great props including his uniform, ID card, tool belt, and large cable truck. The first couple of times, the cops checked his credentials, but after a while, they just waved at him each time they were called to the neighborhood. Just another day in the life of the cable guy.

Soon I shortened the phrase to "Just another day..." and added whatever description was relevant to the story, like "in our terrifying history," or "where black people are not welcome in public spaces," or "driving while black." Friends and readers started sending me news articles so I could post them as "just another day" occurrences.

After Trayvon Martin was murdered, I was speaking to a friend about the case, and she interrupted me and said, "But he was a thug. He was looking in windows, and he had no right to be there."

"No," I said. "You've been watching too much Fox News. He was just a high school boy who happened to be tall and who wore a hoodie. That should not have been reason enough for him to die."

Besides, Ronald and I agreed later when I told him of my conversation, even if he were a thug (and we truly don't believe he was anything but an average high-school kid), did he deserve to be killed?

According to the stereotypes peddled in our country, if you are a young, black male, you should avoid wearing what ninety percent of teenage boys wear every day—hoodies and baggy pants, and you should not be seen driving or going out at night or be seen in the street even in daylight, because you are obviously planning a criminal or violent act. And if a cop or a vigilante approaches you brandishing a gun, you should not defend yourself because, obviously, the white man with the gun has a right to trail you against the advice of the police, or the police officer has the right to shoot you if he deems you are a threat. Of course, he had already decided you were a threat when he saw your taillight was out, or that you were selling loose cigarettes, or standing in front of a store, or playing with a toy gun, or listening to music, or crossing the community grounds with a bag of Skittles and a can of iced tea. As soon as he laid eyes on you, he knew you had no right to be there.

Does America really believe that Trayvon Martin should have been shot and killed for walking back to his father's gated community home, because he was tall, black, and wearing a hoodie? Fifty-one percent of Americans explicitly expressed racist beliefs in an Associated Press poll taken in 2012. Fifty-six percent of Americans responded to the poll and were found to have implicit racist beliefs.

Many of my blog posts are detailed essays, in comparison to my "just another day" Facebook postings, about the killing of unarmed black men and how their deaths and the country's reaction have changed me and how I perceive the way race is played out in America. Not every man or woman killed at the hands of a police officer or vigilante made it into my posts. I would never stop writing if they did, because the list grows longer and longer; however, every single unjust shooting has twisted my heart. This book contains those posts, revised with additional commentary and updates, that did touch on these murders, in the order they were posted to my blog to demonstrate my growing terror at the way black Americans are treated, and to honor and stand by the mothers who lost their children, the ones who are speaking out to try to prevent new members from joining their club, and to the mothers, wives, daughters, sisters, aunts, and grandmothers who suffer grief in silence because they feel they have no voice in America.

To the Mothers of the Movement, I still wish I could have gone over to you at the barbecue restaurant that day and quietly and tearlessly expressed my condolences and thanks, as well as offer you what little comfort I could. But emotions overwhelmed me.

Your courage, determination, and ability to live each and every day in the face of enormous sorrow are beyond my capacity. Your willingness to share your stories in the hope that no one else will suffer such an unjust loss is amazing—you still have the ability to care about what happens to others when it seems no one cared what happened to your son or daughter.

Women of color have historically gone on, as you have, with faith and hope, even when the rest of us cannot imagine how. Americans should be standing by you. We need to listen to your stories and express the outrage they elicit. We must change the narrative of race in America. What we cannot do is to stand apart and be silent, distancing ourselves from racial discourse, as our country is immersed in Trump's era of law and order. It is more important than ever to acknowledge our history of racial oppression and ongoing efforts to perpetuate it and to stand for equal opportunity and equal and fair treatment under the law. Unless we stand together and demand it, post-racialism will never be realized in this country, and, on another day and another and another, more black men, women, and children will be unjustly murdered in America. I stand beside you, Mothers of the Movement, and add my voice to yours.

Chapter 1
Profiling Fatality

Everyone who wasn't a total recluse in early 2012 had heard about the shooting death of Trayvon Martin, a seventeen-year-old black boy from Sanford, Florida, the city in which my in-laws were born and raised, and where we still have family. Trayvon left his father's house in a gated community on February 26, 2012, to run to the convenience store for some Skittles and iced tea during the halftime of a game he was watching on TV. On his way back, he realized he was being followed and called his friend Rachel Jeantel, who told him to run. He didn't, and neighborhood watch coordinator George Zimmerman, against neighborhood watch rules that specify a neighbor is only to be the eyes and ears for the police, caught up with him, confronted him, and shot and killed him.

Zimmerman, identified as white by the police but Hispanic by his family, claimed self-defense under the Florida stand-your-ground law and the Sanford police agreed with him, at least until public outrage changed their minds. Even so, he would walk free for forty-six days before being charged.

Profiling is dangerous, and so is carrying a gun.

I'm married to a black man. I spent many hours in our four decades together worrying if he was safe out there in the world, a world that mostly considers him to be criminal or dangerous based on his skin color. No matter that he spent twenty-five years protecting the citizens of our community as a firefighter. No matter that he is a devoted husband and father. No matter that he is a talented artist, musician, and single-handicap golfer. No matter that he is an ethical man who wouldn't pick up a dime off the street unless it was to return it to its owner. The color of his skin is all that matters when police stop him for DWB, driving while black, or when women lock their car doors as he walks through a parking lot back to his car, or when people treat him disrespectfully or ignore him.

Once when Ronald got home very late, I was angry. "Where have you been?" I asked when he walked into the bedroom. "I was ready to start calling the hospitals."

"I'm going to turn on the light," he said. "I don't want you to be upset by what you see, okay? Then I'll explain what happened."

He turned on the light, and I recoiled from the sight before me. His T-shirt and shorts were covered in blood. His cheek and lip were swollen.

He had gone to Planet 505, a bar on Westcott Street in Syracuse, New York, to hear a band. On his way back to his car, he was jumped from behind and punched in the head. A fight ensued. The other man, a white guy, kept calling Ronald an Arab. When the police arrived, they immediately assumed Ronald was the perpetrator and cuffed him while the white man remained free. At least the white man admitted he had started the tussle, and Ronald refused to press charges. While the inside of Ronald's cheek had been torn when the man grabbed him in the mouth during the fight, the man now had four broken fingers to show for it. The white guy refused medical assistance. Ronald drove himself to the emergency room for three stitches. The man said he attacked Ronald because he was the "Arab man" who had broken into his car. He believed this because that night Ronald wore a Kufi, a hat worn in northern African and some mid-Eastern countries. The assailant profiled Ronald, much like Zimmerman profiled Trayvon because he wore a hoodie.

My husband has a license to carry and conceal a gun, but he doesn't, unless he is transporting his guns to the shooting range for Olympic-style target practice. He doesn't carry them holstered, but locked and unloaded in a gun box in the back of the SUV.

He also is certified to teach pistol safety and taught classes a few years ago. He told me how men walked into class with swagger, and how they sent their wives to class with guns too big for their hands and too heavy for them to handle. Some class members, men and women, mentioned they couldn't wait to shoot someone.

I was appalled by his stories, but he felt he could provide a service: if people were going to own guns, then at least they should know how to use them safely. He added some of his own expertise, for those anxious to shoot someone, about what it is like to react in an extreme circumstance, like firefighting or maybe in the case of someone breaking into your home. Your body wants to flee; your heart is racing; your breath is heaving; your senses are heightened; your fine motor skills leave you, and you lose all accuracy. He wanted his students to know that it isn't easy to make good decisions under such circumstances and that any impulse might be wrong. In addition, he would ask them if they had thought about what it would mean to shoot someone.

Did George Zimmerman ask himself what it would mean to shoot someone?

Zimmerman said he shot in self-defense, but was he brandishing his gun when he approached Trayvon? How would you react if someone approached you with a gun? I think I would be paralyzed by fear. Perhaps you might push him, if you could. Maybe that's what Trayvon did. We won't ever know what happened that night. I wished Trayvon had arrived safely back in front of the TV to catch the end of the game after his snack run, but he didn't because he was profiled, and someone who was carrying a gun acted on a bad decision. Was protecting Zimmerman's neighborhood worth Trayvon's life?

So many gun proponents think we should all carry guns, maybe like the Wild West. But I think only the police and other safety officers should have them. The stand-your-ground law is being considered in the state in which I now live, as is the right to carry in public parks. That scares me. Most people aren't trained the way the police are trained to handle guns and potentially dangerous situations, and bad decisions will undoubtedly change or end people's lives.

I remember the boys my daughters went to school with in our urban school district in Syracuse, New York. In kindergarten they were sweet, creative, and fun-loving, if not mischievous. By eighth grade, some were over six feet tall. They were boys still, but they had man-sized bodies. Already people showed fear around them, particularly the black boys, but to me, they were the same boys with the mischievous smiles from kindergarten.

"Hi, Mrs. Hagan," they'd call when they saw me in the hallway or the parking lot, some with baritone voices. I feared for them in the same way I feared for my husband. How would the rest of the world treat them? I know my fears weren't unfounded. Trayvon validates them. He should have been able to watch that game, eat Skittles, drink his iced tea, talk to his girlfriend, go to college, get married, raise children, and become a productive citizen. Instead, he died. He was profiled and someone had a gun.

When young black men are categorized and profiled, what chance do they have for success? Why can't the world see the sweet faces and mischievous smiles beneath the hoodies? Why can't they see another human being, full of life and potential? Why must our young black men die too soon?

Chapter 2
Profiling Fatality 2: More on Trayvon Martin

When is it okay to use deadly force? My local paper asked that question of its readers in March 2012. The paper, *The Winston-Salem Journal*, printed three responses:

Harvey Pulliam, Jr. said:

I will not seek permission from anyone to use deadly force to prevent bodily harm from being inflicted on either my family or myself.

I shall not seek permission to exercise my endowed rights in using deadly force to repel any threat to my life and liberty, and limb. Be warned that I will not hesitate, if threatened, to exercise any and all of these rights, and use whatever force is necessary to remedy the situation, should it occur.

William Sams said, "When your life or property is threatened."

Louis Jones said:

Citizens should only be allowed to use deadly force if they are facing possible mortal danger to themselves or their loved ones. If they fear for their lives or anyone else's with them at that time, they should definitely feel justified in using deadly force.

Protection of one's self, property and/or family to me is a high priority.

Apparently, we were a threat the day Ronald and I almost got run over by a carful of young white people.

In October 2011 Ronald and I left the movie theater after a matinee. We were holding hands, just like always. There were few people. As a car drove past us, the white male in the backseat turned and stared at us. Then, the white female driver cut the car hard right, pulled up just ahead of us, and slammed on the brakes. We didn't quite know what to think, so we crossed the parking lot behind the car, still holding hands. Suddenly the car turned left, in our direction, and slammed the brakes again. We kept walking, but we heard the tires cut hard on the tarmac, and the car turned directly at us, speeding up, and missing us by inches from behind. I scooted forward but Ronald held his ground, as the guy in the backseat yelled some racial profanity as they drove off.

"People think that doesn't happen anymore," he said as we walked toward our car. But I know it does, and I was scared. It happened just weeks before, when some white teenagers in Mississippi decided they wanted to kill a nigger and they killed James Craig Anderson, a 49-year-old assembly line worker.

I wondered if seeing us together had incited our assailants.

We had just talked about it the night before we went to the movies. We had gone out to dinner, and, as the hostess seated us, taking us past a large table of about ten white diners, we felt their eyes on us. They stopped eating and talking and bore holes through us with their stares. Ronald said he was tired of it. Decades tired.

Most days, it doesn't compute. We don't waste a moment's time caring what other people think, and then it slaps us silly when we aren't paying attention. Like when that car veered toward us.

"I would have taken care of it," he said to me when we got into our car in the theater parking lot. He protects me. He's always done that. He makes me feel safe, assures me he wouldn't let anything happen to me. He has not told me about the things that might scare me, like when he was inside a large apartment building engulfed in flames, and his air hose disconnected. He became disoriented. He would have gone down if one of the other firefighters hadn't slammed him up against the wall and reconnected his hose. I only found out because I overheard him in the other room, weeks after the big fire, telling his dad. But he didn't tell me. He didn't want me to know he could die on the job. He didn't want me to know he could die in the street, just for being a black man.

I was staring out the passenger window as we pulled out of the theater parking lot, trying to calm my breathing, trying to stop my mind from imagining what might have happened. Knowing that he would have kept me safe, but wondering if that would have meant he or someone else would have gotten hurt.

"Don't sweat the one that didn't get you," he said. My heart kept beating against my chest. I won't ever get used to people who hate others so much they have to do something about it. It scares the bejesus out of me. I don't think of people that way, because I don't think that way. But there they are, staring me in the face, threatening assault.

What was it about us, a middle-aged, interracial couple, holding hands while walking through the parking lot, that made that white woman and two white men decide we were threatening? What caused them to use deadly force in the form of a car to pursue us? Is it because we are different?

Or were they a threat to us? Should we have been carrying and engaged in a shootout in the theater parking lot?

Was Trayvon Martin a threat for walking back to his father's house with a packet of Skittles and a can of iced tea? Did that demand trailing him, confronting him, scaring him, and killing him?

Our neighborhood homeowners' association had an e-mail exchange a few days after Trayvon was shot dead. A black man had been seen walking in the neighborhood, carrying a clipboard. "Call the police immediately," one neighbor advised. Another said, "Is he carrying Skittles?"

Even though I was the secretary of the organization then, I refused to engage in the dialogue. It left me feeling ill and wanting to disavow myself from my neighbors. One neighbor, an octogenarian, reported a few minutes later that she had walked down her driveway and asked the man what he was doing. He said he was dropping off flyers for a landscaping company.

What have we come to when people can't walk down the street without being perceived as a threat? What's going to happen when everyone is armed and dangerous in a society that considers things as mundane as passing on the right or driving too slowly personal affronts?

People often perceive threat where there is none. They look at people who are different than they, and their difference scares them. A teen walking down the street, in daylight or at night, is not a threat. Even a group of teens walking down the street is not a threat. People go outside, and go from home, to school, to friends' houses, to the mall, and to restaurants. Sometimes, they just want to walk around. Is there any law against that? Not the last time I checked. What if it were your child with his or her group of friends? Would you want other people to perceive those children as a threat, and possibly use deadly force against them?

Now, if a teen or adult is circling a house, looking in windows, and trying the doors, maybe that person is up to no good, and the police should be called. But does he live there, and he forgot his key? Is it your job to confront him and find out? Of course, sometimes the police don't act as stewards of goodwill, either.

Henry Louis Gates Jr., a Harvard professor, famously returned to his home after a trip and discovered his door was jammed and couldn't be opened. A neighbor called the police because Gates, a black man in his fifties who walked with a cane, looked suspicious. He had lived in the neighborhood for years, but his neighbor didn't recognize him or know him. He was different. The police were confrontational, and Gates lost his patience. After all, he was at home, he was tired from traveling, and he felt the police acted in a racist manner. He was arrested.

I know this about people: they feel most comfortable with others who are just like they are. That might mean they seek people who are ethnically, economically, or educationally the same. Most people won't notice this, but I do, because I am half of an interracial relationship, and I can tell you without hesitation after forty-plus years of experience that we don't fit in most social situations. One of us is often the lone minority in the room. Mostly, Ronald finds himself as the sole black man at a function. Sometimes, I am the only white woman. Or we are the only mixed-race couple in more diverse crowds. Both of us feel comfortable in these situations, but it is hard not to notice other people's discomfort. Suddenly they find themselves wondering what to say, if they are offending someone, or worse yet, they feel offended by us.

Sometimes complete strangers grill us about our life. "What did your parents say?" they'll ask. We are over sixty. Does it matter what our parents thought? Mostly, we end up in a lively question-and-answer session about our life. We don't mind the questions, but it hardly ever ends up that the person asking them decides that he or she wants to see us socially again. The discomfort doesn't go away. We might as well be a goat and a dog walking side by side.

Harsh, I know. I see how dangerous it is to be viewed as different, even if we aren't so different from other couples. I remember that car swerving toward us in the theater parking lot. I remember Trayvon, and I know Zimmerman felt justified using deadly force.

Chapter 3
Profiling Fatality 3: The Demonization of George Zimmerman

I know there are evil people in the world. Hitler comes to mind, and I could list others, but you probably know them already or you have your own list. The truly evil have no regard for human life; they suffer no remorse for their actions. They have no conscience. They feel entitled. They feel justified.

Most people aren't like that. We are flawed, though, and hardly perfect. That's what I wanted to think about George Zimmerman. That he was doing what he thought was right when he abandoned his plan to run an errand and, instead, followed a hooded boy, Trayvon Martin, through his neighborhood. I wondered if he had been exasperated by recent break-ins and maybe he thought he could handle whatever the situation turned out to be. In the last chapter I asked, "Did George Zimmerman ask himself what it would mean to shoot someone?"

I don't know if he ever asked himself that question, but maybe he thought he would be lauded as a hero. I remember daydreaming as a child about what it would be like if I did something heroic, something that everyone would notice and be thankful for. My daydream made me feel wanted, loved, needed, and valued. I think lots of people daydream like that. But Zimmerman got something else when he pulled the trigger on that evening.

He got the weight of killing a teenager pressing on his soul for the rest of his life. He got recognition, not as a hero, but as a vigilante. He put his own life in danger and maybe that of his family when people started threatening him for his unconscionable action. Even if no one ever acts in kind, his life will never be the same.

Later, I would discover George Zimmerman would indeed turn out to be more bad than good. After the trial, he tried to cash in on his infamy. Gun manufacturers and gun groups supported him, including raising funds for legal expenses. Just after the trial, he was photographed with a Kel-Tec worker at their gun manufacturing plant outside Orlando, Florida, where he was given a tour, and where he inquired if he could purchase one of their rifles. He attempted to raise money by selling his paintings of American and Confederate flags that were later proven to be copied from stock photos. He was involved in several Twitter scandals. He auctioned the murder weapon for a purported $250,000. He supposedly saved a couple in a car accident that was later revealed as being set up so he could look the hero. He was arrested several times for domestic violence against an ex-fiancée, his estranged wife and her father, and later, a girlfriend. I was too generous in my depiction of Zimmerman as a man who made a bad decision that cost a boy his life.

George Zimmerman represents the trend of many people wanting to protect their homes, possessions, and lives. Here is an e-mail exchange that occurred when I was the secretary of our homeowners' association: A neighbor e-mailed me back in October 2011 (I have printed the exchange exactly as written, typos, grammatical errors, and misspellings included):

Dianne,

This is XXX and XXX XXX at XXX Lane. Just wanted to make you and the other neighbors aware of the fact we had a house break in on Friday morning. I was at home at the time. I pulled my handgun on him and he fled my residence upon meeting me on the stairs. The suspect matched the suspects that broke into the home last weekend on XXX as well. They are still investigating it and I hope that they catch these theives! They are apparently ringing doorbells and if no one answers the come in. I was upstairs and heard him

*come in...luckily, I spared him his life and he didnt hard me. None
the less, it is so very scarey! Its that time of year an people are looking
for presents and other items.*

*You may want to send out an email to the neighborhood to
just be on the lookout and be very cautious and make sure doors are
locked and alarms are set if they have them!*

Have a good weekend!!!

I was shocked by the e-mail, especially the line where
he (I assumed it was the husband—the couple share an e-mail.
Months later, I discovered it was the wife who wrote the e-
mail, but I will continue using "he" because of how the story
unfolded) said, "I spared him his life." The signature line,
"Have a good weekend!" surprised me, too. It seemed so out
of place, gleeful, in an e-mail that delivered such a heavy
message. But under my obligation as an officer of the HOA, I
e-mailed back and asked him for a description.

He replied, "Black male mid twenties.... scruffy thin
wirery beard/ goatie. Gray hoodie on.... evil looking eyes. 5'9
or 5'10 about 140-150."

Evil eyes? What do evil eyes look like? Were they
blackened out like the demons' eyes on the show *Supernatural*?

Hoodie? That gives me pause. I decided to do some
editing when I sent my message out to the neighborhood. I
sent the following:

*Please be advised that there were two break-ins in our
neighborhood in the last week or so. It appears a black male in his
20s, 5'9" or 5'10", 140 - 150 pounds and with a wiry beard, was
seen in the neighborhood and is a suspect in the two break-ins. The
second break-in, he was confronted by the homeowner and ran away.
The police believe the suspect is ringing doorbells and then breaking
in if there is no answer. Please take precautions and make sure you
keep your doors locked and report any suspicious people in the
neighborhood to the police.*

Be safe!

Apparently, the homeowner was not happy with my version of events. He sent a note to the neighborhood watch leader, and she put this e-mail out to the neighborhood:

From the owner of XXX:

My home, XXX was broken into, not attempted. I met him in my staircase with our GLOCK .45 and he took off running out the front door and around the back of the house. Nothing was taken; he didn't have time because luckily I was upstairs and heard him walking around in my kitchen. The description of the black male is from my eye witness encounter. Not sure if door bell was rung, you can not hear it upstairs. Apparently, when I came home, I didn't lock the door...he pretty much just walked in. Our door handle is tricky...if you lock it, but turn it slightly it will unlock. I'm thinking that is what happened. I always lock the door.

Well, I thought, you ought to spring for a new lock. I was upset that now the neighborhood knew one of the neighbors carried a gun and considered using it against another person. Would the other neighbors view the incident as bravery on the part of the homeowner? Would the rest of them run out to purchase Glocks (easy to do in my state) for household use? Would they buy a few guns: one to keep by the bedside, one next to the TV remote, one in the kitchen drawer, and another stuck in the side pocket of the car door?

Ronald had his own opinion on the matter. He said that if the intruder were a seasoned criminal, a real bad guy, the owner standing on the stairway with the Glock would not have deterred him. Rather, the situation could have been reversed: the intruder holding his own gun and not afraid to use it, or the intruder grabbing the owner's gun. Then, it's the intruder deciding whether to spare a life or end one.

I wrote a personal e-mail to the neighborhood watch leader:

Yes, XXX emailed me the details, but I did not want to put in the Google groups that he brandished a gun. I felt uncomfortable about revealing that point. I'm not against carrying guns; my husband is a competitive pistol shooter and a certified pistol safety instructor, but I am against people brandishing guns when they don't know how to use them or talking about doing harm and so forth when shooting someone is a horrible thing even if the guy had ill intent – it's not a video game or movie. Maybe he wasn't happy that I didn't let the neighbors know of his bravery. And his e-mail was a bit of a jumble – I wasn't sure if he meant his doorbell was rung or if that was what the police said they thought was happening. Anyway, thanks for putting out the correct version. I hope I don't start to see our neighbors brandishing guns while out walking the dog.

She responded:

He/She (not certain which one) emailed me and I asked her if I should distribute her message to the group. She said yes, so I did, but maybe I shouldn't have. I just wanted people to be aware that he had gotten into the house. I also asked how he got in, whether she had heard a bell, and that was her reply.

It is a bit unusual because we've gone so long without any break-ins. Hope it's not a sign of the times.

It is a sign of the times. A sign that as a society we value some lives more than others and property more than human life. We live in difficult and complicated times, but then again, humanity has always suffered by its own hand. What's worse is that we continue to look for bad guys. Right now, they are the ones wearing the hoodies and the ones holding the guns. The definition of who the bad guys are changes with the times, or by political affiliation, religious views, race, and class.

We must stop thinking that everyone else is the bad guy, and realize that we all have the power to be bad as easily as anyone else. All it takes is one bad decision on a rainy night or while standing on the staircase, holding a Glock, and looking down on an intruder.

I don't hate George Zimmerman, and I don't wish him dead. He is not evil. He is not a demon. He is simply human, albeit a bad one. I want to feel sorry for him—sorry that he killed a teenager, and sorry that we all have to live with that.

Chapter 4

More on Trayvon Martin and George Zimmerman by Way of My Husband and the Game of Golf

Trayvon Martin's tragic death receded from the public eye and from public memory just six weeks after it happened. I had to wonder if the public had gotten its fill and decided to move on. It appeared the media had. Perhaps they had nothing new to report. More current events needed to be reported, I suppose. I was saddened that our memories and passion were so short.

I knew George Zimmerman had to be held accountable for his actions that night, but, as noted, it would take forty-six days. I wrote that he is not evil, simply human. That doesn't mean he should be allowed to walk the streets free after what he did. Others out there who think what he did is right and righteous must know that with the right to bear arms comes great responsibility. All freedoms come with responsibility.

What upset me the most is that some people believed the tragedy was not racially motivated. Yes, Zimmerman is interethnic—Caucasian and Hispanic—but we don't know how Zimmerman identifies, and we certainly didn't know his thoughts on race except for what he said on the 911 tape, most of which is garbled. What he considered suspicious about Trayvon is a mystery, but it certainly appeared it was because Trayvon was a black teenager wearing a hoodie.

Every day, black boys and black men are at risk of being identified as suspicious, and that distrust can turn dangerous and deadly within a few minutes.

I can't get out of my head how accurate that statement is, and how intimately familiar it feels when thinking about my life and my husband's experiences.

Ronald plays golf. There is something called a

gangsome here in this Southern state. It's a group of men who play competitively daily for cash. Teams are assembled from a pool of four levels of players. The A player on each team is allowed to pick a B, C and D level player. On the gangsome he joined in 2012, many of the men had played together for over thirty years. They were mostly white. They mostly didn't like him. The few black men on the gangsome were older than Ronald and didn't speak up about how the white men playing alongside them often treated them disrespectfully. They avoided talking to Ronald. They were from down here, and they remembered Jim Crow laws. They knew their place and were either okay with occupying it, or they refused to speak up about it. One of them once told Ronald not to show the white men a photograph of me, his white wife, because "that's not accepted down here."

Ronald was put in the D pool of players. No one bothered to ask him what his handicap was or how well he played. He had played golf, and played well at that time, for over thirty-five years, but the grass down here is different than grass in the Northeast, where he learned to play. The grass in the Southeast is thicker, viny, straight instead of bent, and he had to adjust his game, so his scoring had dropped a little. Though, even with that fact, he should never have been put in the D level and belonged in the B or A level.

The funny thing is, he came home with cash in his pocket every day. Some of the men on the teams he played on had never once made money in all the years they played the gangsome, and, suddenly, after he got on their team, they began winning.

It made a lot of the men angry and suspicious.

"Have they accused you of sandbagging yet?" I asked him when he came home one day and pulled a wad of bills out of his pocket. Sandbagging is when a good player pretends not to play well in order to hustle the other players and take their money.

"No, but they must be wondering," he responded.

"Well, they put you in the Ds; they have to live with it," I said. He didn't ask to be put in the lowest-level skill group.

Some of the men did not acknowledge Ronald, even if they were on his team. They didn't speak to him, even when he asked a direct question. They talked while he hit his tee shot and walked in front of his line to the green when he hit in the fairway. He was invisible, or at least, they wished he were.

"What will happen if they tell Ronald they don't want him to play?" my friend asked me when I related some of the things that happened on the gangsome.

"It's a municipal course. They can't tell him he can't play," I responded.

Other guys on the gangsome rifled through his golf bag when they thought he wasn't looking, and sometimes, when they knew he was.

A few confronted him. One accused him of not putting his money in the skins pot, (or scats, as they call them down here), even though he had. Skins are the cash awards in competition for the lowest score on a hole. If there is no lowest score, the skin gets passed to the next hole and the next, until a player scores lowest on a hole and collects all prior skins not won. For the gangsome, everyone puts ten dollars in the skins pot for payout to the winners.

Another player said Ronald cheated on a hole when he took a ball drop. That white man was on another hole, and he used the f-word with "mother" in front of it. Ronald told him it wasn't his business, and he ought to learn the rules of golf. Then, Ronald told him that he would pull out of the hole if he had a problem, and picked up his ball and took a double bogey. The guy still wouldn't back down. Ronald used the f-word, too, even though he doesn't, usually. He's told me in the past that sometimes that's the only way a white guy will listen.

Another white guy on the other team jumped into the argument. He was sitting in a golf cart, and he told Ronald he came to the course prepared. He announced he had a gun in his golf bag, and he moved to get out of the cart and retrieve it.

Ronald said, "Don't move. Don't get out of that cart. I'm warning you. If you get out of that cart, I will be on you before you ever reach your golf bag." The guy sat back down.

One of Ronald's team members picked up his own bag and walked off the course when the exchange occurred. He hadn't said a word to Ronald the whole time they played. Back at the clubhouse the gangsome leader said, "I heard you tried to cheat."

"Cheat? I don't cheat," Ronald said. Then he explained what happened.

"Oh, well, that part of the course is 'ground under repair.' You could have taken a free drop, no stroke penalty," the leader said, confirming what Ronald already knew. But he didn't say he'd talk to the other guy for spoiling Ronald's round and possibly costing him cash winnings.

The guy who had accused Ronald of cheating slunk through the crowd and left. Ronald stopped going for a few days. He said it was stressful and affecting his game. I told him, "They won. They don't want you there, and you gave them exactly what they wanted." I didn't learn until years later that he had been threatened with a gun. He didn't want to scare me. Had I known then, I wouldn't have encouraged him to go back.

He returned the next day. "You're right," he said. "If I stopped going every place white people didn't want me, I wouldn't go anywhere."

The next evening, I went with him to the course so I could walk nine holes while he played. We ran into a couple of black guys, and they joined us. Ronald said all the black guys come out at dusk and play the course, after the white guys have gone home for the day.

"They sure don't like you, bro'," said one. "All they do is talk about you."

"I told him they don't want him here," I said. "I told him, 'Bad enough you're black; bad enough you are from up North; and bad enough you take their money every day.'"

The guy laughed. "Three strikes against him. But you gotta keep going back. Don't let them stop you."

Another of Ronald's black acquaintances had played on the gangsome a few times. Then, he told Ronald he hated it. "Why do I want to play with a bunch of rednecks who don't want me there?"

I guessed if someone had to do it, Ronald was the best choice. That knowledge scared me, even before I learned one of the men had a gun and was prepared to use it, but I can't keep him boxed and wrapped in tissue paper in the closet so he doesn't get damaged. I've already accepted that as his wife, I might one day find the police knocking on my door to tell me something I don't want to hear. This is America.

He was the best choice for representing on the gangsome because he wouldn't let them get away with anything, just like he didn't let the white guys on the fire department do whatever they wanted and force him off the job. Or when the white seller didn't want to sell the house to us because we are interracial and she said we would ruin the neighborhood. Or when the white car salesman wouldn't let Ronald test-drive the Acura RL because, he said, "You can't afford this car."

Ronald bought the car a week later from another salesman while the first guy watched with his mouth open. He tried to claim Ronald was his customer. "No, I'm not. You didn't want to sell me a car," Ronald said. "And I've spoken to your manager about it."

As we continued on the course, we ended up with another group of three black men. It was getting dark and a storm was blowing in. There was no one else on the course, anyway, so they played as one big group. The other three black men were circumspect at first. I know they were thinking, "What kind of trouble are we going to be in when they see six black men out here with a white woman?"

I wasn't worried. I'd been in that situation before, and whether it's the police or just some "concerned" citizen asking if I am there of my own volition, I have an answer for them. Even as a middle-aged woman, white men still think I've been coerced. They can't imagine that I want to be there. They can't imagine Ronald is my husband.

Once, I fainted at the mall when we still lived in Syracuse and Ronald and I were out shopping. I'm pretty sure it was caused by a hot flash, but no one else seemed to believe me, and I ended up spending the night at the hospital after getting a few stitches on the back of my head where it hit the tiled floor.

It could have been worse, but as I was falling, Ronald quickly reached out and grabbed my hand to mitigate the impact. Then he went into fire lieutenant mode, running the scene until the first responders got there. They were relatively new firefighters, and, even though Ronald was retired by then, they addressed him as lieutenant. They knew him from the job, but they didn't realize he was more to me than a Good Samaritan.

"Can we call someone, ma'am, to meet you at the hospital?" one asked, as they were getting ready to load me into the ambulance.

"I guess you can call my husband, but he's already

heard you. He's right here."

There were a lot of apologies all around.

We got caught in the thunderstorm on the last hole and ran back to our cars. I jumped into the passenger seat, but as Ronald was loading his clubs into the back of the SUV and changing his shoes, one of the other guys walked up to him to say good-bye.

"Don't stop going. You'll just give them what they want," he said.

I have to keep asking myself, "What do white people want?" They want to say they aren't racist, but their actions are often the opposite of what they say. It's easy to tell someone like my husband that he reads into everything and looks for racism. That's an easy way out. No one must change anything about what they want, what they think, or how those two things contribute to racism in America.

What did George Zimmerman want that night?

Trayvon must have known he was in trouble when he saw Zimmerman trailing him. He must have known it wouldn't end well. Did he know that meant the end of his life? Should he have just stayed home so he wouldn't have run into Zimmerman? Understood that white people don't want to see black people where they are, especially at night? Should he have considered their discomfort over his wanting a snack?

It doesn't seem fair to Trayvon, but I suspect his father wished he had boxed and wrapped him in tissue paper and stored him safe in the closet, so the police wouldn't have knocked on his door and told him something he didn't want to hear.

Chapter 5
George Zimmerman Held the Gun, but America Pulled the Trigger

On the website that he created against the advice of his first legal counsel, who later dropped their representation, George Zimmerman said the following:

"I was involved in a life altering event which led me to become the subject of intense media coverage. As a result of the incident and subsequent media coverage, I have been forced to leave my home, my school, my employer, my family and ultimately, my entire life." The website no longer exists.

It *was* a life-altering event, particularly for Trayvon Martin, who lost his life, but also for everyone directly connected, and all of us who aren't. Zimmerman called Trayvon's death "the incident," a phrase that diminished the tragedy. On April 11, 2012, he was finally charged with second-degree murder and taken into custody.

Being charged forty-six days after Trayvon's death was a late first step toward justice, accountability, and responsibility. But America has historically been a lousy steward of positive race relations. We got rid of slavery, and then President Andrew Johnson put a halt to Reconstruction, and Jim Crow rose up to oppress and segregate freed people of color. We got rid of Jim Crow through the Civil Rights Act, and President Richard Nixon came along with the Southern Strategy and the school-to-prison pipeline. We elected our first mixed-race president, and the Tea Party rose up to "take back America" and helped elect Trump. For every positive action, there has been an equal or stronger negative reaction.

We have never had an honest dialogue about how black boys and black men are relentlessly demonized in America. They are portrayed as violent and sexually driven predators, based on a historical fear that white society held about their black slaves hundreds of years ago. This perception gives credence to the paranoia George Zimmerman demonstrated. He was acting based on perceptions and biases widely accepted by white Americans.

Of course, white men have historically been predators. They repeatedly raped slave women without remorse. The children born of this violence were lawfully and conveniently relegated to a life of slavery because their mothers were slaves. Many light-skinned individuals became house slaves because they were deemed trustworthy, compared to the darker field hands. After all, they worked in close proximity to white women and children. Some white women, who recognized familial resemblance in the light-skinned slaves to their husbands or sons, and who perhaps resented their husbands' or sons' betrayal, treated the slaves brutally.

The fear whites had of black men led to beatings and lynching. Civil Rights may have theoretically changed our collective ethical stance on equality between the races, demanding that we strive toward an ideal America, but little has changed. How is shooting less violent than lynching? How was Trayvon walking back to his father's house any more criminal than a black boy whistling at a white woman, as Carolyn Bryant charged, then recanted fifty years later, of Emmett Till in 1955, before he was kidnapped, tortured, and killed? It is unforgiveable Emmett lost his life over a lie, just as it is unforgivable Trayvon lost his life for walking through his father's neighborhood.

We are unable to embrace a post-racial America. Rather, since the election of President Barack Obama, there has been an increased expression of racist ideology and actions, not just from fringe groups, but also in mainstream America. Nowhere is this clearer than in the election of Donald Trump, the man responsible for promulgating the birther conspiracy. We have left our best selves behind while allowing old racial paradigms to thrive.

I know this because I've lived it for over forty years as the white spouse in an interracial relationship. I see how insidious racism is. I see how often whites unconsciously express racist sentiments and get defensive if they are called on it. I see how hopeless black members of my family feel because it is soul depleting to be treated as a skin color, not as a person, with the full weight of having dark skin in a white world bearing down on them every hour of every day. I am not exaggerating. I have to say this, and I hope you will listen. Ask yourself what stereotypes you harbor about people who are a different race than you are. Question your perceptions and ask if they are based on reality, or on emotional bias. Striving to change those perceptions could create a safer world for all of us.

It breaks my heart when I see people who don't bother to get to know my husband. They've decided who he is the moment they lay eyes on him. They will never know his quirky, random sense of humor, his creative and artistic spirit, his sensitivity and empathy, and his ability to study, focus, and excel in his profession as a fire lieutenant, as a musician, an artist, and a golfer. They won't care about his driving need to serve the community when he put his life on the line every single time he showed up at the fire station for twenty-five years. They won't believe that he is a dedicated, loving husband and father. They will never know how their fear, or even worse, their contempt, has burned a searing scar on his soul.

They will also never know how they disappointed and frightened me, like the time forty white men ganged up on Ronald at the bowling alley because they didn't think he should be dating me.

Ronald joined a men's bowling league with a white

friend of ours in the early 1980s. We had known him since undergraduate school, and we are still friends today. His wife, also white, and I decided we would go watch the men bowl. Almost immediately, one of the white men on the opposing team started making comments about me, like, "What's she doing with him?" and "She'd be better off with me."

At first, I thought it was funny. Ronald was in his twenties, a firefighter, a musician, and an artist. He dressed handsomely and neatly. He was of average height, but he was physically fit and cut. The white man was older and overweight with a beach-ball-sized belly. He wore a T-shirt stained with food and dirt, needed a haircut, and drank to excess. I wondered aloud what made him think I would choose him over Ronald.

The more he drank, the bolder he got, and the more his teammates egged him on. When Ronald got up to bowl, the man purposely distracted him. He stood close to me, invading my space. I grew frightened, and Ronald became frustrated and angry. Then the man said something to Ronald that I could not hear. Ronald picked up a nearby beer bottle and smashed it on the table edge, holding the jagged top like a weapon. Suddenly, I lost sight of him. A group of about forty white men had swarmed him.

I pushed my way through the men, my heart pounding. One of them had his arm around Ronald's neck, and others pushed their faces into Ronald's and shouted profanities at him.

"Stop it," I screamed, pushing at the men surrounding Ronald and trying to pull the man's arm from around his neck. I felt swallowed by the mass of bodies. Many of the men towered over me, and I could only see their chests and stomachs in the fray. The strong odors of alcohol, tobacco, and sweat turned my stomach. Terror raced through me, bright lights flashing in front of my eyes. At that moment, I realized our relationship could move some people to violence. "Stop, please! Let go of him! Why are you doing this?" I cried looking at the faces around me. Some of the men, their eyes looking at the floor, backed away.

"Let go of me. We're leaving," Ronald said. The man let him go and he walked through the others to get his bowling gear. The men started wandering back to their alleys. The guy who had grabbed Ronald around the neck stood in front of me. He was tall and imposing.

"Why did you do this?" I asked him, my voice squeezed by disbelief. "Didn't you see what your teammate was doing?"

"I guess it wasn't right," he said.

Our friend and his wife stood planted, side-by-side, looking puzzled.

"Should we leave, too?" he asked Ronald.

"Do whatever you have to do," Ronald answered, his breath heaving.

"I know a few of these guys. One of them is a neighbor. He's a nice man."

"He's nice to you," Ronald said, picking up his ball bag and turning away. I followed him to the exit. He held the door for me, and, as I stepped through it, I turned back to see our friend packing up his equipment. Outside, Ronald opened the trunk to put his ball bag in the car, and he picked up the tire iron, testing its weight.

"Don't," I said.

Ronald looked at me and held the tire iron out in front of him. Then he put it back in the trunk and closed the lid.

We got away, but I will never forget the terror I felt that night.

People feel entitled and righteous in their biased certainties. They will never understand my fear of the violence they may perpetrate against us, like the time two white men, empty beer cans littering the bottom of their motor boat, rammed our canoe out in the middle of a lake that suddenly seemed larger and deeper than it had before. They laughed as their hull barreled toward the canoe end where I sat, and I stuck my arm out to deflect the full impact.

I don't want some strange white men to feel possessive and protective of me, a dangerous kind of misogyny. I chose my life partner, my soul mate, because I love him, so far beyond the color of his skin or mine. Not that I ever felt white in the sense it is portrayed and perpetuated here in America, as a nonethnic, nonracial, middle-class persona, the imitation vanilla in the spice cabinet, but in the sense that I am of European descent. I gave up family, friends, privilege, and entitlement for my relationship, and I don't regret it.

What I regret is how we Americans ignore our racially divided society and depend on perceptions based on emotions and stereotypes, and how our willful ignorance abetted George Zimmerman the night he shot and killed Trayvon Martin. He held the gun, but America pulled the trigger.

Chapter 6
Diminishing Racism, One Granite Countertop at a Time

Often, I make a note of how many times race appears in news stories in a given week. An example was one week in April 2012. Here is a quick recap, details to follow. George Zimmerman was released from jail on a $150,000 bail to await trial. He apologized to Trayvon's parents in court, and many people believe the gesture was opportunistic, and, now, knowing him better, it appears that may have been true. A North Carolina judge, Greg Weeks, tossed out the death sentence of inmate Marcus Robinson because he ruled the trial was influenced by racial bias. It was the first ruling under the North Carolina 2009 Racial Justice Act. Two black men filed a discrimination lawsuit against TV shows *The Bachelor* and *The Bachelorette* for the treatment they received during a casting call. They believed the shows intentionally screened out people of color.

The moral side on which you fall in each of the above events doesn't matter. What matters is that they happened, because racism, bias, and discrimination still exist.

Robinson, a black man who killed a white teenager in 1991, deserved a fair trial and to be judged by his peers, but the prosecutors rejected qualified black jurors and stacked the jury pool with whites. It may have been a fair trial in every other way, but even so, because bias was used in jury selection, we'll never know for sure. That uncertainty was enough to throw out the death sentence under the 2009 Racial Justice Act. This law was passed in North Carolina, (Kentucky is the only other state with a similar law on the books), because of the number of black inmates on death row in comparison to white inmates.

The judge's ruling stated, "Race was a materially,

practically and statistically significant factor in the decision to exercise peremptory challenges during jury selection by prosecutors," and that the disparity was enough "to support an inference of intentional discrimination."

Cassandra Stubbs, one of Robinson's attorneys, said, "For over 100 years, jury selection in capital cases has been plagued by racial discrimination against qualified African-American citizens. Today's decision offers promise that change in this area, long overdue, is finally coming."

The two men who filed a lawsuit against the popular reality series said that they were treated differently than white applicants. One was asked why he was even at the hotel where the casting call took place. This happened to Ronald once at a golf tournament held in New Haven, Connecticut. The hotel clerk assured him there was no way he had a reservation and sent him across town to an inexpensive hotel in a predominately black area of the city. The next day, Ronald returned to the hotel and demanded to speak to the manager, who ended up verifying his reservation and giving him a free night for any inconvenience he suffered. During the week of the tournament, he was mistaken for a valet, and hotel staff tried to prevent him from going into the private events scheduled for the tournament. Apparently, they didn't think black golfers were welcome.

The suit goes on to claim that TV programs assume "minorities in lead roles and interracial dating [are] unappealing to the shows' audience."

It says, "The refusal to hire minority applicants is a conscious attempt to minimize the risk of alienating their majority-white viewership and the advertisers targeting that viewership. Nevertheless, such discrimination is impermissible under federal law."

The Bachelorette cast Rachel Lindsay as its new lead in 2017. She was the first black lead in the history of the program, where controversy over its homogenous cast continued over the years since the 2012 lawsuit was filed. The cast was the most diverse in the history of the show. Almost half of the thirty-one contestants were people of color.

When the announcement was made, people reacted. One said in an e-mail to blogger Reality Steve, who blogs about reality TV, "It's a bad idea because to be honest, I don't see Rachel getting the viewership they are used to. I don't see it ...The only reason they are giving it to her is because she is black. They are just filling some quota and hoping that this will shut everyone up for a few years and once people start complaining again that there isn't a black bachelor or bachelorette, then they will simply cast another one."

Another e-mail addressed to Reality Steve said, "I'm sad it will be Rachel. In general, I don't find African-American women as attractive."

Change is slow, but the season premiere numbers, although down slightly from 2016, held steady.

Zimmerman's bail hearing made headlines. When he gave his apology in court, Trayvon's parents were stoic. The prosecutors called the gesture opportunistic, but Zimmerman insisted he wanted to apologize to them in private but was advised not to. He also stated he thought Trayvon was older, as if that made a difference, but he didn't say specifically what caused him to follow Trayvon, or what made him look suspicious.

Here's the thing about racism or any "-ism": most times, they are subconscious reactions. It's ingrained. It's a lens through which we process and interpret what we experience and see. We have to work hard to adjust that lens and accept other possibilities. But first, we have to acknowledge that our biases exist and that we operate under their influence without question.

"Why bother?" some might ask. "What does it have to

do with my life?"

I have heard that question many times. Once, I participated in a diversity workshop sponsored by my then-employer, and I shared some of the situations Ronald and I had experienced. Many people expressed shock, even sorrow, that such things still occurred, but one white man just shook his head.

"What do you expect me to do about it?" he asked, sounding disgusted. "I don't have anything to do with it, and I've got my own problems."

Then he said, "What do you think of your Louis Farrakhan? He's against interracial relationships, too."

That was the first time I realized some people considered me nonwhite, perhaps even black, because of my relationship with Ronald, and because I bore his children. That proved to me conclusively that race is a social construct, because it appears one can move back and forth between races depending on who is looking at you. President Obama suffered this bias, and so have my daughters.

Before I could respond, one of the other workshop participants, a white woman, stood up. She had something important to say and wanted to make sure she was heard.

"I've known Dianne since she was a college student," she said. "I can vouch that she is a very nice person."

Her comment was meant to diffuse, but instead, I was upset that she felt my character needed defending, as if she were saying, "Okay, you're right, she made this terrible choice, but she's still likeable." Yes, yes, I'm a nice person, but is that the only reason someone should care about the discrimination I've experienced by being in an interracial relationship? Even nasty people deserve equality and fair treatment.

Another white woman in the workshop said, "You should consider yourself fortunate, because interracial marriage used to be illegal. At least you were allowed to marry."

That comment made me angry. As if I needed permission to marry and should be happy I received it. Just ask any gay couple if they were waiting for permission to legalize their relationship. They didn't want or need permission. The Supreme Court agreed in June 2015.

There aren't many houses without television or the internet these days. According to Nielsen, 95% of homes in America have access to television and, according to Pew Research, 73% have internet access. I admit to watching TV shows with regularity and passion in some instances—I can feel my anticipation for *Call the Midwife* escalating as Sunday evening approaches. I have my favorites.

It is difficult to get Ronald's enthusiasm aroused for television programs, but a show on the History Channel in 2012, called *Full Metal Jousting,* caught his attention, so we watched the eight episodes together. It was a reality show that resurrected the ancient Eurocentric sport of riding a horse toward an opponent, dressed in armor (both the rider and the horse), and carrying a large lance, which is aimed at the opponent in an attempt to unhorse him. The show highlighted a competition that ended with one jouster being the overall champion and winning $100,000. There was not a single black contestant or trainer on the show.

"I've noticed there aren't any black competitors," said Ronald while we were watching one of the first few episodes, "but I still want to watch it. I wonder, though, did any black guys audition, or were they not drawn to the sport?"

I had noticed, too. I can't imagine that there are no black horse trainers or black theatrical jousters or black rodeo cowboys (or Asian or Hispanic ones, for that matter). Those areas of expertise were overwhelmingly the backgrounds of the all white competitors. Then again, Cara, Mackenzie and I used to go to the Renaissance Faire in Sterling, New York, and there were very few black actors there and not many black spectators. Ronald fought us for years about going, thinking he wouldn't like it, but Mackenzie and I convinced him to go in 2011, and he had a great time. It may even have inspired his interest in jousting. I digress.

In my quest for diverse television, I find myself gravitating to HGTV. Seems ridiculous, right? But the shows are quite diverse—all kinds of couples and singles looking for housing, in all price ranges and geographic locations, to buy or rent. Seeking housing can be an equal opportunity endeavor as long as the seller, the landlord, or the realtor isn't biased, as was the case when we purchased our first home. Perhaps the cameras prevent such bias. After all, who wants to be caught red-handed unless that person is a member of a racial extremist group?

Watching people of every ilk search to fulfill one of the basic human needs, shelter, is in some way comforting to me. The universality of the need normalizes the process and breaks through cultural and racial differences. Right now, it seems everyone, no matter race, gender, sexual orientation, age, or socioeconomic level, wants granite countertops and stainless-steel appliances. How mundane is that?

In many ways, TV and the internet give us more shared experiences and shared aspirations, like those granite countertops. Advertisers create the need, just as they did when we were raising our daughters and minivans became a must-have for people with children. The message is spread via television and the internet, and the fulfillment of that created need is equal opportunity, as long as there is economic access. Even then, depending on your budget, you can buy granite-looking Formica or granite tiles at Lowe's or select a high-quality, unique piece at a granite yard.

Where the disconnect happens, and where the

situation can turn ugly, is that now, as we begin to congregate in the same places, to want the same things, to do the same things, and to share the same experiences, biases and social constructs crop up and get in the way.

It happened in 2015 on the Napa Valley Wine Train in California, where a black women's book club, Sistahs on the Reading Edge, was ousted from the train because white passengers complained their laughter was too loud. At the next station, they were led through the train cars while other wine tasters watched. Then they were left on the station platform, where police officers waited for them. A hashtag #laughingwhileblack became popular after the humiliating incident. Tweets followed, like these two, to explain the disconnect: "If you're not following the norms of white people, then it's inappropriate & disrespectful," and "I hope [wine train] knows that black people like wine and can afford it, too. Not just white people, women in particular." Their lawsuit against the Napa Valley Wine Train was settled in April 2016.

We need to keep questioning ourselves; to realize no one needs permission from anyone to be who they are or to act in certain ways or be certain places; and to understand that bias and discrimination of any sort hurts everyone, not just the targeted person or group. We have to acknowledge the lens through which each one of us views the world is not the only lens and does not afford the only picture of things, but is just one view out of billions. We have to learn to speak up when bias is evident because even if it doesn't seem to affect you, it does. It affects all of us. We need more sharing of experiences and aspirations, like those granite countertops and the wine train, so we can see our commonality. Only then, perhaps, race won't be in the headlines every week.

Chapter 7
The Door of No Return

In 2013 as the right increased its rancorous cries against President Obama and George Zimmerman's trial played out on television, I found myself unable to write for weeks. I tried. I had pages and pages of words strung together, but none of them seemed right. None of them expressed precisely what I wanted to say. None of them captured my moodiness, sense of urgency, restlessness, sadness, and discomfort. I couldn't put a finger on it, let alone write about it.

My dreams were strange—secret missions, magic, journeys, Ricky Ricardo (not Desi Arnaz), mystery, murder, and chaos. They were an every-morning occurrence in the quiet before my alarm sounded. Some mornings, I was relieved by the beeping of the alarm, and other days, I wished to slide back into my alternate universe.

Most of my conversations and posts to Facebook back then, as now, were political in nature. They centered on equal rights, and immigration, and the Supreme Court's decisions, and reproductive health, and jobs, and healthcare, and scandals, and gun laws, and the Democrats, and the Republicans, and the liberals, and the conservatives, and the poor, and the wealthy, and the minorities, and the majority, and the great divide in our country. The fissure grew exponentially during this time and set the conditions for the divisiveness we are experiencing now in the Trump era.

Sometimes Ronald says, "I know how much you want to talk about this (or that), but I can't anymore. Not right now. I've lived this stuff my whole life. It hasn't changed."

He's right. I understand how it can become overwhelming, how it can blot out what little light we have during our time on this earth, because that of which we speak is darkness, and hatred, and separation, and blindness, and ignorance, and judgment, and intolerance.

Can we alleviate ignorance? Sometimes, ignorance is willful. We've seen it in defense of fake news outlets like Breitbart News and InfoWars, while large media outlets like CNN, *The New York Times*, and *The Washington Post* have been assassinated by the right as liberal news media. The defense of the Confederate monuments is willful ignorance, and I saw it on my Facebook page weeks before the Charlottesville, Virginia, protests and tragedy, when friends were discussing the removal of the Confederate monuments in New Orleans.

"You shouldn't erase history," one said in defense of keeping the monuments right where they were.

I didn't want to respond at first. I knew how it would go, but neither did I want to be silent. I explained that history should be taught in classrooms, the real history of that time, including the states' secession papers, many of which listed slavery as the cause for secession, and there should be no monuments to those who committed treason. His other friends ganged up and told me the Civil War was not about slavery, no one was charged with treason, and that what I said was wrong. I responded that Lincoln had been assassinated and Johnson, a Southern sympathizer, rescinded many mandates of Reconstruction. Another poster said she often bought Confederate trinkets at a store owned by a black man, as proof that people of color support the Confederacy, too. I wondered if she would fall for the logic that if one white man decided murder was acceptable, that would mean all white men believe so, too, but I kept that thought to myself. Another said I offended her and disparaged her heritage. Did she care she offended me? The poster of the original message told me to post on my own page—"Bye." Even though I knew him professionally for almost twenty years, I left his page and ended our friendship.

Can we erase hatred from a person's mind? I believe it is learned behavior, but sometimes I imagine it is organic, almost genetic, perhaps inherited like one's ethnic knowing, the legacy of the family migration pattern, and the lore of the family and the group from which it emanates. It's powerful in that it blinds one from seeing another way, perhaps a better way or more righteous way, and it causes one to lie, and to make excuses, and to blame the target of the hatred. I've felt the sting of this narrow way of thinking when a few white Southerners have claimed their heritage as the cause for their beliefs about race and supremacy, as if the option of thinking differently is not an option at all. They've called our marriage an abomination and told us such relationships are not accepted down here, yet we've seen many interracial relationships since moving South.

Why is it common for some people to believe the following: Poor people are lazy. They don't want to work. They feel entitled and want free stuff. Black men are suspicious, dangerous, and criminal. Women need strong white men to make their reproductive health decisions. Women don't own their bodies. Women do not deserve equal pay for equal work. Minorities do not need doors to be opened in the workplace or at institutions of higher education by the law of the land, because they are not qualified, anyway. Gay people are bad and sinful and an abomination, and they could change if they wanted to. Illegal immigrants want to steal our jobs and our country. Muslims are terrorists and jealous of our freedoms. Americans are white, and able, and smart, and fair, and deserving. These beliefs seem more ominous and dangerous considering the many Trump executive orders that he claims were put in place to fulfill campaign promises made to his base. I only hope our three branches of government can work the way there were designed to prevent him from deconstructing our democracy, yet I had dispensed of all hope until we elected the most diverse Congress in the history of our country in the 2018 election, including Congresswoman Lucy McBath, Jordan Davis' mother.

I am a woman. I am white, ethnically Irish and Italian. I am a Christian with no church affiliation, though I spent my first twelve years as a Catholic and a year or two as a Lutheran. I grew up poor and lived on welfare for a short time in my childhood when my father had a heart attack and the doctor was not sure if he could return to work. I'm married to a black man descended from slaves. I am identified as white when I am alone. I am identified as unacceptable or an abomination when I am with my husband. I made a terrible error in life when I married Ronald nearly four decades ago and gave birth to mixed-race twins, at least according to some who feel no shame in letting us know what they think. Like the time we were crossing a store parking lot and a white man, his wife and three children in tow, kept looking at us and shaking his head. We could see his anger escalate at the sight of us, his muttered comments becoming louder and sharper in tone, as he rushed his wife and children away from us.

We looked at one another after they had attained a safe distance. "What was that all about?" I asked. Ronald joked about the possibility that interracial relationships were contagious, and the man didn't want his wife or children to catch what we had.

I remember the 1970s, when I met Ronald freshman year of college. The possibilities seemed endless. The feminist movement had taught me I was equal to men. The civil rights movement meant that we were all equal under the law. It was a new day, and we were unafraid even when people reacted angrily toward us, because we wanted to believe it was just the individual, that the collective thoughts on gender and race had changed.

Forty years later, I know it isn't just the individual. It's a collective paranoia and attitude and hatred and fear and anger and wielding of power that fuels discrimination. It's a system engineered to benefit some while disadvantaging others. It's the collective trashing of whole groups of people, and of individuals. It is the deafening silence of the horde that feels no outrage. It is the hurtful reality that no matter what, if you are not part of the majority, you are at risk of being judged differently, and unkindly, and harmfully, and dangerously, and fatally.

We are moving backward quickly, and harshly, and violently. The movements that propelled women and minorities closer to equality, begun so many ages ago and fought and died for over generations, are stalled, and there is opposing momentum to push them backward. Donald Trump's record validated this push.

And the effort to push us backward gets more vicious as the stakes go up, and the groups behind the pushback are more open about their intent, proud of their intent, strong in their conviction that some are more equal than others, and are more entitled to enjoy this great country.

When we go one step forward toward equality, we are pushed back three steps. The 2013 Supreme Court decision to strike down the Defense of Marriage Act versus the Supreme Court decision to strike down parts of the Voting Rights Act - one step forward, three steps back. The proverbial ink was not even dry, and the ones who believe some are more equal than others started the process to make inequality the law with racially motivated voter suppression legislation, quickly enacted before elections took place. States like North Carolina, where I live, spent millions in taxpayer dollars defending such unconstitutional laws. Even though the North Carolina districting has been struck down by the Supreme Court twice for relying too heavily on race in drawing the districts, and a federal appeals court charged the state targeted "African-Americans with almost surgical precision," the state legislature continues to search for ways to ensure the state remains solidly red in its voting record after turning blue in 2008 when Obama won the state, Bev Purdue (D) won as governor, and Kay Hagan (D) was elected as Senator. That was reversed in 2012, and there are very few Democratic elected officials at the state and federal level today, although more than a few of the larger cities have Democratic mayors, and we have a Democratic governor Roy Cooper, who wields little power due to the GOP-controlled state legislature that passed laws limiting his executive powers.

Voter suppression efforts continued in the 2018 election. The 9th Congressional district in North Carolina was unable to send a representative to Congress due to a charge of ballot harvesting, where it is alleged paid individuals went door to door and offered to drop mail-in ballots for absentee voters at the post office. Instead ballots were found altered, forged, and some were suspected of being tossed. The North Carolina Elections Board refused to certify Mark Harris, the GOP candidate, who was ahead of Dan McCready, the Democratic candidate, by 905 votes. Harris demanded McCready concede, but McCready refused and filed a lawsuit. Harris remained resolute, even after suffering two strokes due to a blood infection and finding himself up against growing evidence of fraud committed by his campaign, including his son's testimony that he counseled his father not to hire Leslie Dowless, who ran the fraud operation. Harris finally relented, stating, "It's become clear to me that public confidence in the 9th District has been undermined to an extent that a new election is warranted."

The Board of Elections voted unanimously to hold a special election in autumn 2019. Until then, the seat will remain vacant. Harris then withdrew his bid a few days later citing health issues and throwing his support to Stony Rushing, a Union County Commissioner and the owner of the Take Aim Training Range located across the border in South Carolina. More Republican hopefuls are stepping up, as of publication. Indictments were filed against Dowless alleging illegal possession of absentee ballots, obstruction of justice, and conspiracy to obstruct justice.

Back in 2013 I was offended by Paula Deen's tearful apologies on television after she lost her partnerships with several companies, including Wal-Mart, Smithfield, Target, Home Depot, and the Food Network when former employees charged she was racist. I was offended she wanted me to believe she was the victim. I was offended she wanted me to tell her it was okay if she expressed her racist thoughts or that she took credit for cuisine that was stolen from enslaved people, or that she peddled a quick path to diabetes and obesity. I was offended that many Americans believed she had a right to believe that people of a different race are inferior. I was offended that these same Americans claimed it was their heritage that made it righteous.

I was angry Paula Deen used her celebrity and wealth to protect her empire when her words and actions were so damaging, not just to the people they personally harmed but to our country, which struggles to live up to its best ideals every day and every hour. I was angry that her book sales skyrocketed when the story broke, and I was flabbergasted by one comment on the Wal-Mart website, posted in response to Wal-Mart severing its partnership with Deen, "Way to go in supporting a fellow Southerner."

What about all the Southerners who are descendants of slaves?

I was offended that some people believed Trayvon Martin didn't have the right to walk to his father's house in the rain. They believed he didn't belong in that neighborhood, much like the neighbor I wrote about in chapter two, who sent an e-mail to the neighborhood, saying there was a suspicious black man walking the streets and carrying a clipboard. So scary! He was only doing what countless other people working for small businesses do— handing out flyers about his business, but because he was black, even in my multicultural neighborhood, it was assumed he was there with ill intent.

I was offended by the cross-examination by the defense team of Rachel Jeantel, Trayvon Martin's friend, who was on the phone with him just seconds before he was shot and killed by George Zimmerman. I was offended by the defense team's culturally insensitive questions, including making comments about her ability to understand English, one of the four languages she speaks, but not her first language, and their effort to discredit her testimony, and her intelligence. The defense team latched on to something Trayvon told her when he realized he was being followed. He described Zimmerman as "a creepy-ass cracker." Later he said, "...Nigger is still following me." As the defense team examined Trayvon's character at the trial of his murderer, they painted him as the racist, rather than a terrified teen.

I was angry that hardly anyone asked if Trayvon feared for his life as he was pursued by an aggressive stranger who did not identify himself and who meant to do him harm. If someone were following you, wouldn't you be fearful, and possibly use strong language to describe the person?

I was angry the GOP said the striking of the Defense of Marriage Act will bring society to a stop. Their actions and support of President Trump will halt society long before equality will.

I was angry that many white Southerners felt compelled to comment on my forty-year-old interracial relationship often and offensively. I was angry that many white people consider themselves racial experts, although they have spent their lives pretending they are race-less while assigning those they consider racial by describing them as other and different and negative. They had conversations about how people of color are racist, like the George Zimmerman defense team accusing Trayvon of racist comments. They blamed the victims of racism instead of the perpetrators and perpetuators of it, the people who believe the victims don't have the right to be in public spaces in America.

They felt self-righteous, not righteous, in their stance. They are horrible, mean-spirited, vicious, discriminatory, small-minded, dangerous people. There, I've said it. It doesn't make me feel better. It makes me sad, and angry, and frustrated, and disappointed, and tired.

President Obama and his family visited the Door of No Return in Senegal in June 2013. Millions of men, women, and children passed through this door and onto ships that transported them to the Americas where they were sold into slavery. I could only wonder at how powerful a moment that was for him, as I was struck silent just viewing footage of it in the media.

For millions of people, lying head to toe in the bottom of ships, many dying from hunger and unsanitary conditions, this journey must have seemed like hell, and, yet, such a horrible, inhuman fate awaited them upon landing. As a country, we refuse to address our hand in it and the awful legacy that is still evident in race relations today. The Obama family visit to the Door of No Return was prescient, given the 2016 campaign and President Trump's election to president. I was stunned by Ben Carson's description of slaves and the way in which his words altered the race narrative by diminishing the atrocity and legacy of slavery: "There were other immigrants who came here in the bottom of slave ships, worked even longer, even harder for less. But they too had a dream that one day their sons, daughters, grandsons, granddaughters, great-grandsons, and great-granddaughters might pursue prosperity and happiness in this land."

That's why my words left me in June 2013, and why they have continued to leave me on many days since the onset of the Trump presidency. I need my words to help me make sense of this time in which we find ourselves.

Chapter 8
To Trayvon, with Love

Dear Trayvon,

I spent the night crying after the George Zimmerman verdict was read on July 13, 2013. I wished, Trayvon, that I had never learned your name, never heard it uttered by reporters or shouted by protesters, because then, you might still be alive. Your parents would have spent your late teenage years worried about your grades, or that you didn't take out the trash, or you were late for dinner, or whether you would choose a college close to home or far away. Instead, they grieve the loss of their son and all the important life events and the mundane moments they won't get to share with you.

I am so sorry we let you down on the night you died. I am so sorry you and your family did not receive justice.

I signed a petition seventeen months before the trial ended, when I first heard about your death, your murder, Trayvon. I wrote five posts about you in the weeks after the press reported your murder, attempting to allay my grief, trying to sort out just how America found itself at this place in our history, where people not only carry guns, but use them and then get away with murder, and at this place where being a black male is still dangerous, and is often fatal. I spent weeks following Zimmerman's trial as if my own life depended on it, and, Trayvon, it did. I am the white wife of a black man and the mother of mixed-race twin daughters, so I understood keenly how this verdict could have made life safer or more dangerous for people of color in this country. In the years since, it's been proven to be more dangerous for men and boys of color.

My husband Ronald and I got home the night of the verdict, and the first thing I did was turn on the TV and flip through the channels, looking for an update on whether the jury had come to a verdict, and within minutes, I saw the breaking news banner at the bottom of the screen. Ronald and I held our breaths while the court reassembled, all except for your parents, and I felt their absence, though I understood why they were not there. I knew I would not have been able to hear those words as your parent. My heart broke for them as they sat through the trial after a stranger, who made a fatal decision, ripped you from their lives.

While we waited months for justice to be served for the taking of your life, another boy, Jordan Davis, was shot and killed for being a passenger in an SUV in which loud music played. He was another child ripped from his parents' arms; another child who would never reach his potential; another child who was not seen as a person, but as a skin color; another child who died because of the stand-your-ground law in Florida, which states that a person, who believes his life is in imminent danger, does not have a duty to retreat and has a right to stand his ground and defend himself. This law bestows Kool-Aid courage to anyone wanting to use his gun for nefarious purposes. Unlike the verdict in your case and others, Michael David Dunn, the man who murdered Jordan, was convicted of first-degree murder and sentenced to life in prison, plus ninety years—a shallow victory in the fight for equality, and little comfort to Jordan's parents.

I could only shake my head as the Zimmerman verdict was announced.

"Five white women," Ronald said. "I told you they'd acquit."

I hadn't wanted to believe that the all-female jury would acquit George Zimmerman. I wanted to believe, all along, that Zimmerman would stand up in court and ask for the lies to stop, as first his mother, then his uncle, and then his father testified that the screaming on the 911 call was his voice, and not yours. I wanted him to admit that he had made terrible, fatal choices that night based on his own biases and hatred, and that those choices will forever echo through history as a reminder of our inhumanity. But he didn't.

Ronald thought I was naïve. I was.

I began to cry when he told me there is no hope for black people in America. There is nothing left to do, nowhere to go, he said, because nothing will change. I believe so much of what he says, because he has such wisdom about these things, but I know in this case, Trayvon, it was his survival as a black man in this racist country, despite his many brushes with other people's potentially fatal decisions, in stark contrast to your short-lived life, and Jordan's short-lived life, that left him full of despair.

"We can't give up," I said, sobs choking my words.

And I won't, Trayvon. For every George Zimmerman out there, let there be three, or four, or eight, or thousands who learn how to see you, and all black boys and men, as the person you are, not just the color of your skin. Let there be ten, or a hundred, or a thousand, or millions who know that you belong and have a right to belong, and who will fight for your right to belong at the store, in the rain, on the walkway, in the gated community in which your father lived, in Sanford, in Florida, in the United States of America. You belonged here. You had a right to be here. Zimmerman was in the wrong place and doing the wrong thing. He acted like a thug that night, because thugs are people who have ill intent and who carry weapons to hurt and kill others, and it doesn't matter what their skin color is or what clothes they wear, because that isn't what makes them thugs.

We failed you, Trayvon. Not because your parents didn't talk to you the way Ronald talked to our daughters, just as his father talked to him and his siblings, and his grandfather talked to his father.

"You can't do what they do," Ronald told our daughters. And I know your parents told you that, too, because they were good and loving parents and they wanted to keep you safe from a country that hates you because of the color of your skin.

We failed you, because we allowed the rising tide of racism to crash over our country unabated. We failed you, because we let gun legislation pass, both federally and at the state level, that supports irresponsible gun ownership. We failed you because some people are privileged in our society while others are not, and some laws seem written to protect only certain citizens while they are used against others. We failed you, because we sat on the laurels of the civil rights movement and grew complacent. We failed you, because George Zimmermans exist everywhere in this country, and will continue to profile black boys like you and Jordan and shoot to kill them.

We won't fail your memory, Trayvon. You will be remembered, as your family lawyer, Benjamin Crump, said the night of the verdict, and "forever remain in the annals of history next to Medgar Evers and Emmett Till as symbols for the fight for equal justice for all." Yet it is no comfort to hear this in a country where systematized racism and racial bias put the lives of black men and boys at risk. Nor does it undo the heinous act that took your life, or fill the hole it seared in the lives and hearts of those left behind.

Know, Trayvon, that there are white people who understand systemic racism. Not all of them, not even half of them, probably not even a third of them, but there are white people, like me, who understand that black Americans do not experience America in the same way white Americans do, because we have been fortunate or unfortunate enough to witness what you experienced as, in my case, a wife, and mother, and daughter-in-law, and sister-in-law, and aunt, and friend.

I, for one, will pledge to fight on your behalf.

I signed a petition for the federal government to reopen its suspended investigation the day after the verdict. I wrote the following comment:

This is a socially important case. It cannot be the precedent that it is okay to shoot and kill black boys because they are perceived through the lens of racism. Trayvon Martin did nothing different than millions of other boys his age do every day: he went out to buy a snack and was talking on his cell phone as he walked back home. He had a right to be there. George Zimmerman had no right to profile him from a distance, pursue him, not identify himself [to Trayvon], and then shoot Trayvon at point-blank range in the heart. Please investigate this fatal act, which denied Trayvon his fundamental civil rights, and his life.

Know that men like my husband, though crushed by the disrespect and humiliation they endure in their lifetimes, as they trailblaze the way toward equality, will continue their fight for justice, even at their personal peril. They will push through their depression and weariness because they don't want other boys to experience what happened to you. They want it to be better, like when my father-in-law moved from Sanford, Florida (where relatives still live), up north so his children would not grow up under Jim Crow laws.

And white people like me will be at their sides, just like whites marched beside Martin Luther King, Jr. We know it is wrong. We believe you when you tell us how it is for you as a black boy living in a racist country. We've even experienced it vicariously, like when the Southern white man stood in our garage when we had a neighborhood yard sale a few weeks before the verdict was read, and told us how all blacks live off the government. He said that standing in the garage of our newly constructed home, looking directly at our

Infiniti G37S parked in the garage along with Ronald's motorcycle, and our CRV, and our daughter's Mazda 3 parked at the curb so our driveway would fit the lawn tractor, refrigerator, and chandelier we were selling. I guess they were all bought with food stamps, Trayvon, because, according to him and many other white people, all black people are on the dole and too lazy to work. I slipped into the house, and Ronald told the white man, "You have to go now."

What if someone else had been there the night George Zimmerman decided you didn't belong in his neighborhood, even though it was obviously multicultural and multiracial? What if just one person had stepped out of his or her house and said to Zimmerman, "You have to go now. Let this boy return safely home. He belongs here."

Trayvon, we will continue the fight for the right of all Americans to belong, to be equal under the law, and to be judged by their characters, and not their physical features or clothing. We cannot rip racial bias from a person's brain, but we can pursue justice, fight the good fight for equality, and remove racism from our institutions, our systems, and our laws.

But what I still wish, Trayvon, is that I had never learned your name, never learned Jordan's name or Tamir's name or Darius' name, never heard them uttered by reporters or shouted by protesters, because then you, and they, might still be alive.

With love and hope,

Dianne

Chapter 9
Outraged

As the right continued to murder Trayvon's memory, pass laws that were constitutionally questionable, and mock President Obama's impromptu talk on race in America, I was left frazzled by incredulity and outrage. Trying to make sense of it all, I put together a list of things we must learn to do to become a rational, compassionate nation that supports equality of all its citizens. This list is needed more than ever under a Trump presidency.

1. Stop. Stop hating. Stop blaming. Stop thinking some people, like you, are better than others. We are all guilty of it. Understand that although there are truly bad people, most of us are just trying to live, imperfectly, which is the most any of us can hope for. Just because someone doesn't look like you or share your perspective, beliefs, or way of doing things, that doesn't mean they are a bad person deserving your hatred. If you cannot stop hating, do everything in your power to make sure you do not act on it, because acting on it does make you a bad person.

2. Learn empathy. We all face adversity at some point in our lives. Money does not save you. Smugness and superiority do not save you. Nor God, if you believe, who promised to save you in the afterlife, not in this one. Learn to feel compassion for the person who is down and out. We need to take care of each other, because the world is completely objective when bad things happen and doesn't pick and choose who will be affected, so every person deserves compassion. Besides, one day it will be your turn to face adversity and the care and understanding of others will help you through it, just as you will have helped others in their time of need.

3. If you are white and you think racism goes both

ways, the most important role you can play in the conversation about race is listener. You've already given your opinion one time too many, and it was off base, offensive, ignorant, untruthful, and dangerous.

4.   If you think you know what it is like to be black in America, and you are not a person of color, stop right now. You have no idea what it is like to be black in America. I have spent more than forty years of my life with a black man, and my children are biracial, yet I do not know exactly what it is to be black. I will never know, because I will never be black. Period.

5.   If you are a minority, any minority (black, Hispanic, female, LGBTQ, Muslim, a person with a disability), even though it may feel scary and difficult, speak up when someone is being offensive. Let people know, as kindly as you can, that what they said is damaging to you, to them, and to society. If you don't tell them, they'll only keep on doing what they are doing and tell the next person they offend that their [black, Hispanic, female, LGBTQ, Muslim, person with a disability] friend doesn't feel as they do, so that next person must be wrong. Be the first to let them know their thinking is wonky, and then offer to help them understand. If they don't want to speak to you after you tell them the truth, that's their loss.

6.   If you hear anyone speak disparagingly about another, whether it is about our president, or the black child walking home from school, or the Mexican family waiting in line at the grocery store, or the little girl who is overweight, or the gay or interracial couple who want to enjoy an evening out, tell them you do not agree with them and ask them why they are so mean-spirited. Then wait for them to answer. I wrote this in 2013, when President Obama served our country. He continually demonstrated graciousness, compassion, intelligence, and rational thought in his actions

and words, and when people spoke disparagingly of him, their comments were often irrational, racially biased, and directed at what they claimed was his illegitimate status. I cannot say the same for President Trump, who often uses his position to disparage groups, individuals, and businesses that do not support or agree with him. He lies, repeatedly. He clearly demonstrates racial, class, and gender bias and ignorance, and he relies on white nationalists and supremacists to advise him. In his case, we need to call his actions and words exactly what they are and not normalize his lies, exaggerations, and biases, while still honoring and respecting the office of president. In fact, it is our obligation as citizens to do so.

7.   Report abuse, harassment, discrimination, and favoritism to your employer, the business you are paying for goods and services, at school, at church, or anywhere else it happens, or else how will it ever stop? This is for every person, even if you were not the receiver of the action. Peer pressure can positively affect people, too.

8.   If you do not consider yourself a racist, stop voting Republican. The party has been recruiting racists since Nixon, and they are more and more blatant in their appeals to hatred, fear, and paranoia to keep the country divided and to advance their agenda, which benefits the wealthy and creates a plutocracy. We witnessed how Trump, his campaign, and his administration embraced hatred and division, the culmination of which unleashed mob-style attacks against protesters at his rallies and unprecedented increases in hate crimes committed against blacks, Muslims, Jews, and transgender individuals.

9.   If you do not consider yourself a misogynist, see number 8.

10.   If you do not consider yourself a homophobe, see number 8.

11.   In fact, if you believe all people should be

equal under the law, see number 8.

12.　　If you are a fiscal conservative, stop lying to yourself. History shows that the Republicans tend to grow government and increase the deficit. See number 8.

13.　　If you are truly a Christian, stop supporting laws and policies that hurt the poor and the underserved. See number 8.

14.　　If you are pro-life, help the children who have already been born, and give women equal access to quality reproductive health. You will see the number of abortions shrink to almost zero. The number of abortions decreased under the Affordable Care Act, because women have access to reproductive health and birth control. See number 8 and write your representatives to stop the assault on the Affordable Care Act. It needs fixing, not replacement.

15.　　If you know for sure that corporations are not people, see number 8.

16.　　If you are female, or identify as an ethnic minority, or are a person with a disability, or LGBTQ, see number 8. They only want your vote, and they will not represent you.

17.　　If you believe socialism is scary and dangerous, you need to think again. The roads you drive your vehicle on, the sewer system to which your home is connected, the police department, the fire department, the military, Social Security, the Center for Disease Control, the Food and Drug Administration, Medicare, Medicaid, and unemployment benefits are just some of the socialist programs in our country. You benefit from those programs, as should all citizens.

18.　　If you believe the Affordable Care Act, or Obamacare, is a socialist program designed to assist people who don't deserve assistance, see number 17 and number 2. Also know that it is good for society overall that people receive proper health care, because it will prevent the epidemic spread of diseases, allow people access to primary care instead of going to the emergency rooms, which should truly be for emergencies, help the hospitals serve their patients better, and keep people healthier overall and not burden society. Health care is a right, not a privilege, and people who tell you it is a privilege do not believe all Americans are equal.

19.   Vote. Vote in every election, including local elections. People died fighting for the inalienable right to vote, so the very least you can do is read up on the issues and the candidates and get your ass to the polls. If you vote, you have a right to complain and ask for representation. If you don't, shut up, because you are part of the problem.

20.   Help someone else vote. Drive people who don't have transportation to the polls. Hold their place in line if they are too old or too tired or too infirm to stand there and they need to sit down. Hold polling officials accountable if they do not provide voting access to people with disabilities.

21.   Do not be a one-issue voter. If you only vote on one issue you are voting in candidates who may have terrible agendas, and they are exploiting your fervor.

22.   If you think murder is wrong, stop supporting stand-your-ground laws, and let people all around you, including your gunmonger friends, know that stand-your-ground is simply a legal workaround to commit murder, and you are going to expend your energy getting the laws repealed and fighting for more stringent gun control laws. Then run, before they shoot you.

23.   If you believe your child deserves to be safe at school, at home, and in your neighborhood, then support the same for other children who live in your neighborhood or attend your child's school, and those who live in different neighborhoods and attend different schools. Find a way to personally support that belief.

24.   Do not paint a group of people with a broad brush based on one attribute, like skin color or socioeconomic status. Every person is an individual, and if you want to be treated as an individual, you ought to treat others the same way. All white people are not the same, and that is true of everyone of every ethnicity, race, gender, and socioeconomic class.

25.   Understand that this is America, and all Americans, as well as people who are visiting, going to school, or working in America, have the right to be where they are: walking down the street, standing on the walkway of a community, buying Skittles at the convenience store, and going home to watch the second half of the game. Stop thinking some people are more deserving of our freedoms than others. We should all enjoy the freedoms we share as Americans, and you should fight hard for that concept, or else one day, you may find yourself on the wrong side of freedom.

26.   If you are a man, treat women as your equals, not as sex objects, property, or baby vessels. Don't engage in sexual harassment nor turn a blind eye if your colleagues do. Stop supporting legislation that takes away women's control over their bodies and sexuality. Fight for equal pay for equal work. Don't support the sex industry, because it exploits young women.

27.   If you are here in America because your family immigrated or took refuge here sometime before or since the birth of this country, support immigration reform. If you don't support it, you are a hypocrite, and perhaps you should follow your own advice and go back to your country of origin, if it will take you.

28.   Do not spend one dime to support the economy or tourist industry of red states that pass laws that are constitutionally questionable, discriminatory, or punitive against certain people, let businesses buy their politicians and

political leaders, treat some of their citizens as less than equal, and allow their citizens to be irresponsible gun owners. Your children will grow up just fine if you don't take them to Disney World.

29.   Teach your children to care for others and to have empathy and compassion for people who are different from them. Empathy is our greatest equalizer, because it opens the mind and squashes irrational judgments and biases.

30.   If you are white, teach your children about race and ethnicity. People of color already do this because they have to for the safety of their children. Talk to your children about your family's ethnic heritage so they will understand everyone is ethnic. Tell them about white privilege and discrimination and that they are unfair and everyone should be treated equally in every circumstance. Teach them to challenge privilege when they benefit because of it, and that it is much more rewarding to earn merit based on hard work and accomplishment, rather than having it handed to them.

31.   Stop watching and reading news sites that report news with a slant, e.g., white supremacy. These sites lie, exaggerate, or alter facts, and push conspiracy theories to sway your thinking. They are counting on you to reach the conclusion that anyone who doesn't look and think like you is dangerous and attempting to take away your freedoms and way of life. Recall the 2016 election conspiracy theory that Hillary Clinton was running a child sex ring at the Comet Ping Pong pizza shop in Washington, DC. A North Carolina man showed up at the shop with an assault rifle to rescue the children he was sure were being held there. There weren't any children, and, fortunately, though the man fired his gun twice, tragedy was avoided. If you must continue to visit these sites, be a critical thinker and make sure you check other sources to verify stories. A story that does not appear in news

media outlets like the nightly news or the major metropolitan newspapers is most likely untrue. The charge that news media are biased and only report stories that fit their liberal viewpoint is also untrue, because they profit by reporting the news, not by hiding it, and pretending otherwise is how these sites keep you from checking the veracity of their stories.

32.   Stop thinking you are a real American, and anyone who isn't exactly like you is not. Anyone born here or who goes through the process to become a citizen is a real American. Our country evolved from a group of people who wanted to discover, conquer, and possess, into a country that willingly takes in people who seek a safe harbor or who dream about a better life. Celebrate our diversity and understand that America's varying faces and perspectives make it a great country.

Chapter 10
Biased Much?

The following letter appeared in my local newspaper in August 2013. It was titled *Racism*.

In response to the letter ('a terrible message" July 28) criticizing the woman holding the "We're racist & proud" sign, I am an American with European heritage. Because of my political and social views, many would label, and have labeled, me a racist. I would argue that I do not deserve that label.

My great-great-grandfather shed blood to free an enslaved people and my family and I have always opposed any measure that would promote one race over another. For example, I think it would be an outrage for a group with European heritage to promote advantages for themselves and call their group the National Association for the Advancement of Anglo-Saxon People. That would be offensive to many of non-Anglo descent.

A European History Month would be similarly offensive, as would an event celebrating White Repertoire Theater. If 12 million Europeans or their families had gained illegal entry into the country, resulting in a drain on the public treasury, I would be opposed to granting them amnesty without consequence.

Again, because of those views, I will be labeled a racist by many screaming racism, because of? Racism. There is no way to escape the label and I am proud of my views promoting equality for all people who obey the law.

If the Rev. Al Sharpton were to call me a racist, I'd never convince him that he is wrong. All I can do is to tolerate, even embrace, the label and proudly continue to hold and express my views.

BARTON TIFFANY

The woman in the photo referred to in the letter was later identified as a leftist who planted herself in the George Zimmerman support rally.

The central fallacy of this letter writer, and many

others, is that everyone, no matter one's ethnic or racial heritage or the color of one's skin, is treated the same. In the writer's view, everyone experiences social interactions and situations equally, and enjoys equal protection under the law. He believes we all have the same experience as citizens of the United States of America. That assumption is wrong, dead wrong in many cases.

Let me illustrate. Male teens of all races dress a lot alike. That's part of adolescence—they are rebelling against the older generations, but conforming to their own generation while claiming they are fiercely independent. They like hoodies and pants that sit low at the waist or below the butt. I don't like the style, but I seem to recall not too many adults of the generation above me liked the short skirts, platform heels, hip-hugger bellbottom jeans, and midriff shirts I wore back in the 1970s, like everyone else my age.

That same uniform takes on different meanings depending on whether the person wearing it is white or black. A white teen might be described as finding himself and sowing his wild oats; it's what ALL boys do, all white boys, anyway.

Put that same uniform on a black teen, and he is a criminal.

Subconscious racial bias and racism are alive and well.

And that's scary, because when a stranger is sizing you up and subconscious racial bias is operating, a black teen may find himself in a fatal situation just as Trayvon Martin did, and Darius Simmons, aged 13, who was shot and killed by his neighbor on May 31, 2012. Patricia Larry, Darius' mother, witnessed the shooting. Can you imagine watching someone kill your child? It is inconceivable.

She testified, "He told Darius that he's going to teach him not to steal, and he shot him." Darius had stolen nothing.

No one should discount the real consequences of

racism and racial bias. They are deadly!

So, when I read a letter like the one above, or someone writes a comment on my Facebook page, or says something in a conversation that diminishes or denies the effect of racial bias, I react.

I have seen how dangerous it is, and not just in the news.

For example: the seller of our first house decided not to honor our contract after she found out we were an interracial couple; forty white men jumped Ronald at a bowling alley because they didn't think he should be able to date me; in college, a group of us resigned from our work study jobs when an administrator fired Ronald after he said people had complained about seeing the two of us together; two white men rammed our canoe with their motor boat because they didn't like seeing us together; a car of twenty-something white kids hurtled toward us as we left the movie theater and one kid yelled a racial epithet as they sped off; a white cop held a gun to Ronald's head as he unlocked his car door because "blacks don't own foreign cars;" a police officer asked Ronald if he was the gardener while he was doing yard work at our house and demanded to see his license when he told the officer he lived there; Ronald was fired from his first job after college because his manager didn't like seeing us together; Ronald was arrested for walking down the street when the police claimed they followed footprints in the snow after a supposed complaint that someone was peeking into a second-floor apartment window. I could list hundreds more situations, and we are just one couple.

I am saddened by it, too. Racial bias is insidious. When I see a black male child, I see a child. I don't see a person who has evil intent, or who can physically take me, or who wants to rob me. I see a child.

When our twin daughters were in first grade, we

separated them so they would be able to develop independently. Mackenzie was shy and relied on Cara to speak for her, and Cara would have forgotten her head at school every day if Mackenzie wasn't tracking behind her picking up her lunchbox, and gloves, and books, and boots.

Cara came home each day to excitedly tell me about her new friend. I went to school one day for a special class project, and, as we waited for the kids to return from a school function in the auditorium, I started a conversation with another mom who was white. We were each delighted to discover the other was the mother of the child who was our daughter's new friend, and we started talking about play dates.

The kids returned, and Cara ran over to hug me. I guess, when the mother discovered Cara was biracial, (neither of us had met the other's child before that moment), she was surprised. She physically backed away from us. During the class project, she and her daughter sat at the same table as we did, because the girls wanted to sit together, but she avoided speaking to me, and I could tell she was comparing her daughter's artwork to Cara's and pushing her daughter to do better. I was saddened by the way the afternoon unfolded.

The next week, Cara came home from school crying. She said her new friend had left to go to another school. I asked the teacher what happened, and because we had known each other for quite a while, she was honest with me when she told me the mother said she was removing her daughter from the school because there was not a single child in the classroom she considered a peer of her daughter, not a single child she would invite to her home, and there were too many black boys in the class, making me wonder how many was too many. I knew the black boys she talked about, and I thought they were wonderful, like I think all children are. Their eyes gleamed with the excitement of learning. Their bodies moved with energy and passion. They were friendly, and funny, and engaging, and creative, and smart. I never saw them as different from my children, but she didn't like my child, either.

I wonder if I had been more like that mother, would I have been frightened, too? I don't think so. I learned from an early age about being open to other people, even if they appeared to be different. Maybe I learned it because I felt like such an unlovable being, and I hoped others would be open to seeing me if I were open to them. Maybe I always had deep empathy for others, that rare ability to walk in someone else's shoes. I wish I could endow others with that kind of compassion. I would travel the country and touch the foreheads and the hearts of people everywhere, so they, too, would see, not through the lenses of hatred and paranoia, but through the lens of acceptance.

I must wonder about someone who can look at a 13-year-old boy and see an enemy, especially when so many white, middle-class children seem to have extended childhoods that last into their mid-twenties and, sometimes, even later. How, then, can one assign a black boy adult power and the wherewithal, and the prowess of adulthood? Racial bias.

There was a story in the *New York Times* in 2013 about white Missouri parents being upset that black parents were transferring their children to better-performing schools. Why would you be upset that someone else desires better educational opportunities for her child? Wouldn't you do the same?

One black mother, who chose to transfer her daughter from a school that had the worst disciplinary rating in the state to a predominately white school with a better disciplinary rating, watched a televised town hall meeting about the school where the "parents angrily protested the transfer of Normandy students across the county line, some yelling that their children could be stabbed and that the district's academic standards would slip."

The mother said, "When I saw them screaming and hollering like they were crazy, I thought to myself, 'Oh my God, this is back in Martin Luther King days. They're going to get the hoses out. They're going to be beating our kids and making sure they don't get off the school bus.'"

Can you imagine wondering if you made the right decision to put your child in a better school and worrying about her safety? The irony of the white parents thinking the same thing is not lost on me. But I have to wonder how their thinking got to that point. Why are they assuming that having black children in their school, in particular, lower-socioeconomic black children, will put their own children in danger? That's what privilege is: protecting that to which you feel entitled and not letting others have access to it.

George Zimmerman thought like that when he shot and killed Trayvon Martin. That's the same kind of thinking John Henry Spooner, whose house had been broken into and his guns stolen, had, when he shot and killed Darius Simmons. He said, when the judge asked him if he felt bad for killing his next-door neighbor, "Not that bad."

When he was questioned on the stand he said, "I wanted my guns back. I just, you ever want something so bad...yeah."

What? His guns were worth more than a child's life? A child who did not steal his guns? A child who was his neighbor and whom he knew? How does anyone come to this?

I can't see us having a conversation on race when the very people who need to be active listeners shut it down before it begins with their disbelief that racism exists. The truth is in the news every day, and in the lives of millions of people of color.

The reason most white people think there is no racism is that they have not experienced it, and they cannot imagine that such horrible things happen in a country where they feel safe and free to live their lives, until, that is, someone of color moves into their neighborhood or attends their child's school.

Chapter 11
There I Was

The government shutdown in 2013 was inevitable. The extreme right, the Tea Partiers, the wacko birds, made it happen. They held the country hostage. They said it was the debt ceiling, and they wanted to defund the Affordable Care Act, or what they referred to as "Obamacare." They continued to vote for a repeal of the ACA under the Trump administration, effectively erasing the legacy of President Obama, in spite of strong bipartisan support for it. When even their most staunch supporters wanted to keep it, and the GOP lost so many seats in Congress after the 2018 election, they quietly dropped their effort to repeal it. But in 2013, they used the ACA as rationalization for the real reason they shut the government down.

Let's start with D. Whiteman. D. Whiteman is the personification of the way individuals who believe they are not at all racist dispense of racism. As he sees it, his intelligence and drive, not a society constructed to give advantage only to certain people, got him where he is. He feels compelled to tell people of color everything he knows about the world that he thinks they don't know. D. Whiteman is essential to this story.

For example, why is it that D. Whiteman felt perfectly comfortable walking up to my husband, Ronald, to start up a conversation that began: "I don't like your president. I'm not racist, but I hate him."

It happened the day after the shutdown at the golf range. The range owner called Ronald "black Ron," and Ronald regaled me over the years he hit balls there with stories of all the things the old white guys felt perfectly comfortable saying to him.

On that day, Ronald was hitting balls and talking with another black man who had been a college basketball player. In his early sixties, he was just a couple years older than Ronald, and they were hitting it off when D. Whiteman, who was down on the other end of the range, walked over and broke into the conversation.

"Why did he do that?" I asked Ronald as he recounted the story a second time, at my request, the day after it happened.

"He wanted to know what we were talking about," Ronald said in response to my question.

What's the thing some white people dislike about people of color who may or may not be recent immigrants to America? Their first language may not be English, and they may communicate with family and friends in their native language. Some white Americans demand people of color conversing in a different language to speak English or "American." I recently watched a smartphone video of a white man named Mike, who was a wheelchair user due to injuries received at war, at an airport gate shouting racial epithets at a Puerto Rican man, who was sitting nearby with his mother and speaking Spanish to her in a private conversation. After Mike tells him it is a crime to speak a different language in America, the Hispanic-American man says, "I'm just as American as you are, Mike." He also explains that many members of his family served in the military and lost limbs, too, but that does not calm Mike, who continues to rant, aggressively and loudly. Mike leaves and returns, a few times, and twice hits the Hispanic man for recording the exchange. Then Mike implores to all the other people waiting at the gate, "Somebody, help me. This guy is fucking attacking me." Mike grows increasingly agitated, even after his wife tries to intervene many times and also asks the Hispanic-American man to stop talking. Airport security, bidden by a couple of other travelers, finally arrives on the scene. When one is bestowed with societal privilege, it is easy to believe that the only thing people of color who speak a different language could possibly be talking about is the white American who can't understand them. The whole world revolves around D. Whiteman.

When two or more black men congregate, that same white American believes they are up to no good. That is what D. Whiteman was thinking when he walked down the range to break up the conversation between the two black men.

Ronald and his acquaintance gave each other a look, but let the white man talk. Soon, it turned bad.

First, the white man was instructive about golf. Ronald had played for over thirty-five years at the time, and he took his range practice seriously. With the range owner's permission, Ronald would set out targets at certain distance intervals. Then he would go through a series of exercises: hitting high, medium, and low; moving the ball five yards left or five yards right of his intended target; landing on the target, behind the target, in front of the target, or making the ball roll up to the target.

A retired fire lieutenant who served his upstate New York community for twenty-five years, Ronald went to the range near our new home in the South just about every day until a few years ago, when his interest changed to bass fishing. That posed an issue for another white man at the range who said, "How do you afford to come here every day? I bet you are on the dole." Ronald could have asked, "How do you afford to be here every day to see me?" but he didn't.

A single-handicapped golfer, Ronald was better than good. He took years of lessons and studied the sport in depth, including the physics behind it. He has built custom golf clubs for himself and others. A lot of people at the range would ask

Ronald for golfing advice, and he generously gave them his time and attention. He loved the game that much.

Why would D. Whiteman believe he could teach Ronald about golf, especially when he wasn't asked?

Because he assumed he knows more, and Ronald knows less.

Then D. Whiteman defended his Second Amendment rights and trashed Obamacare. Ronald disagreed with him. D. Whiteman said, "You don't understand the concepts."

Why did D. Whiteman think Ronald was not capable of understanding?

Because he assumed he is smarter, and Ronald is dumber.

Ronald looked at the other black man and said, "Excuse me, I have to take care of this."

"Do what you have to do," the black man told him.

Then Ronald went there, deep into the darkness of rage—where he recalls the countless times he put his life on the line as a firefighter to save someone who did not believe Ronald was the officer in charge at the fire scene, or someone who said he didn't want a "nigger" in his house even though it was burning down, or someone who didn't want a "nigger" to perform CPR on his wife, even though she was dying.

He blasted D. Whiteman, called him a motherfucker, and asked him who he thought he was. Back in the seventies, when we met freshman year of college, he would have said, "I hooged out."

Ronald was silent when he got home. He went straight up to the man room. He came out only to go into our bedroom, where he sprawled sideways across the bed, and pulled a blanket to his chin.

I cooked dinner, called him to come eat, and we ate in silence. I told him after I cleaned up that maybe we should go to Lowe's and buy a new cabinet mounted microwave, because ours broke. We drove in silence. I knew something had happened.

I was glad Lorne was working in the appliance department. He's a black man from Pittsburgh, and he and Ronald talk a lot, sometimes for hours. As he showed us microwaves, Ronald let it out.

"There I was, just being black, and along comes D. Whiteman."

Lorne laughed. "I hear you, man."

As the story came out, a detail at a time, I didn't say much. He needed to tell it uninterrupted. He needed to be understood by someone who, like him, had experienced the same thing over and over.

When I did speak, I said, "This is why just about every middle-aged black man I know suffers from depression."

"Yeah, you're right," Lorne said, nodding.

You are a black male in America. You survive childhood and your teenage years, where your chance of dying jumps into double digits. You go to college and graduate. You survive your twenties, which include run-ins with the police for DWB (driving while black) and you don't get shot or end up in jail, at least not for more than a night while they decide if they can charge you or not. You get a decent job serving your community. You get married, have children, and raise them with love and compassion and warnings about what it is to be black in America. You stay with your wife, even when the job is killing you and your white colleagues are trying to drive you away because they think blacks don't deserve to work there. You try like crazy not to let that darkness creep into your marriage or cause you to fail on the job. You hang in. You put up with the bullshit. Finally, you retire. You reach that age where you think the bullshit won't happen anymore.

But it does. It happens when you step out the door and some white yahoo wants to tell you about yourself: "I was worried when you moved into the neighborhood that you couldn't afford the house," or how the Confederate flag is about Southern heritage, and not racism. It happens when you turn on the news and, for eight years, watched Congressional bullies try to knock down President Obama because they couldn't stand a black man in the highest office of the land, and, later, people shouting, "Make America great again," and giving Nazi salutes, while black citizens were being killed in the streets by cops, vigilantes, and white supremacist terrorists; and now Trump and his administration of supremacists enacting executive orders about law and order directed at people of color, and Muslims, and immigrants. You start wondering how much longer you have to put up with it—the racism, the contempt, the hatred, the paranoia, the potential for violence, and the sense of entitlement with which white Americans walk around. You get bombarded with it every single day.

That is what it is like to be a middle-aged black man in America.

It has pained me to be a witness to this or a target, as I was one summer evening, when, after dinner, we decided to sit on a bench located on a busy downtown street to enjoy the weather, like many other couples and singles. A white man asked whether we minded if he sat on the bench directly across from us. We said he was welcome to sit. Once seated, he declared us an abomination. He quoted Bible passages and said he was going to call the police on us. Did he know the Supreme Court banned miscegenation laws in 1967?

Or like the time we sat at another spot downtown, eating Jimmy John's subs and enjoying the weather, and three white bicycle cops pulled up next to us for almost half an hour, making me wonder why they weren't off doing their jobs, and why they felt comfortable parking so close to us. Finally, one mounted his bicycle, pedaled by, and, looking directly at me, asked, "Is everything okay this evening?"

Or like when I discovered in a national newsfeed that the attorney who represented our neighborhood homeowners' association was the state chapter chairman of the League of the South (LOS), a known white supremacist/secessionist hate group on the Southern Poverty Law Center hate watch list. The LOS wants to subjugate, deport, or kill all people of color and whites who are not ethnically pure. As president of the homeowners' association, I brought this information to the other officers, and both averred that people are allowed their strong opinions, and they did not think said opinions would interfere with his service to our diverse neighborhood. They accepted my resignation in lieu of replacing the attorney.

Sometimes I am bewildered by the situations in which we find ourselves. I wonder why complete strangers feel entitled to judge our forty-year relationship. Other times I am terrified, as I was in the theater parking lot when those white teens aimed their car at us, or at the bowling alley when the forty men attacked Ronald. Mostly, I am outraged. I am outraged these incidents still happen with regularity, forty years after my parents and I stopped speaking because they disapproved of my relationship with a black man, and thirty years after we wanted to buy our first home and had to file a discrimination suit to get it.

I am outraged that America is in denial of systemic and institutional racism and white privilege, and instead, chooses to criminalize and dehumanize a group of citizens.

I am angry I cannot change people's biases and make life better for the person I love unreservedly.

I think President Obama must have felt very much like Ronald and millions of other black men during his presidency. Why were they attacking him? Why were they attacking laws that the majority of Americans supported? Because they thought he didn't understand the concepts; because he cannot achieve their definition of American, as a mixed-race individual; and because they are confident whiteness makes them more capable, smarter, and better.

I don't know how President Obama put up with it for eight years without losing it, without taking care of it, and without calling them motherfuckers. He was careful to mostly keep race out of the conversation. But the race card had already been pulled from the deck by the GOP, its supporters, the racist crazies, and D. Whitemen, who ranted and raved about Obama and his legitimacy, and who still feel perfectly comfortable letting every black person they see know what their opinion is of him, "your president," as if he only represented black people, not all Americans; and what they think of you, because their opinion matters and yours doesn't. In response to eight years of feeling unrepresented, even though the Senate and Congress had GOP majorities, they elected an incompetent narcissist who is bent on erasing everything accomplished in spite of unprecedented obstruction under Obama's administration, and they are quick to tell you that Trump is president now and he will make America great again. They mean white again. Trump represents the very worst of D. Whiteman.

I feel Ronald's depression press against my heart when he says, "I know you understand a lot of it, but I am the one out there being bombarded, and I am tired. I can't do it anymore."

That's why I don't break the silence when he doesn't want to talk. It's why I can barely write sometimes because I've been through it over and over, and I've written about it this way and that way, but nothing changes.

President Obama must have felt it when the extreme right called for his impeachment because they believed his presidency, and even his citizenship, were illegitimate: "There I was, just being black, and here comes D. Whiteman."

President Obama is one of the millions of middle-aged black men in America who waded through the bullshit and danger, only to discover, despite being elected the leader of the free world, that he is still trapped by white entitlement and privilege. Like all black men of retirement age, retirement did not save Barack Obama from D. Whiteman.

I know the real reason for the government shutdown in 2013.

Chapter 12
Race War

My heart broke—again—when Michael Brown, Jr. was gunned down in Ferguson, Missouri on August 9, 2014, by police officer Darren Wilson in broad daylight, in front of many witnesses, his hands raised. I was outraged, devastated by the loss of one more life in this racially broken country.

The community reacted: some in solidarity and peace, others through looting and violence.

How did the authorities react? With tear gas and rubber bullets and increased military presence.

I believe that individuals who are rendered powerless by the color of their skin (or their gender or their socioeconomic class), and who cannot trust the very people sworn to serve and protect them, sometimes resort to violence out of desperation. What's left to do when just living may prove fatal at the hands of authority? Or when the authority targets poor communities and uses police stops as a source of revenue through the imposition of fines and late fees, causing many individuals to fall further into poverty? It doesn't seem right or productive to most people, particularly to those who live in the privileged power group, but I understand it.

We are experiencing the systemic erasure of one race of Americans through an unjust and prejudiced judicial system, a privatized prison system, unequal educational opportunity, a growing underclass of working people, usurpation of rights and freedoms, geographical containment, media stereotyping and omission, and now, the threat of a law-and-order mandate under a Trump administration.

Vigilantes and some police officers murder men and boys of color (and, increasingly, women and girls of color.) Sworn to protect and serve? Not certain police officers, and certainly not vigilantes like Zimmerman, or supremacists like Roof.

We've lost the ground we gained after the 1964 Civil Rights Act. The trend is clear. Jim Crow may have hibernated for fifty years (I rather think he operated under cloak of darkness), but he is up and about and ripping and running unbridled through communities of color. White supremacy made its way back into mainstream society during Trump's campaign. A seemingly large portion of those who identify as white Americans, particularly conservative thinkers and voters, don't want to talk about it. Why? They support it. They vote for it. They demand it. They participate in it by arming up and acting on paranoia, hatred, and fear. They don't believe it affects them or their communities. They claim it's their heritage, a heritage and history of conquering, oppression, and genocide. Others simply don't believe race disparity exists.

There is a race war, but it isn't the one to which the GOP and extreme conservatives are alluding.

"This is a part of the war on whites that's being launched by the Democratic Party. And the way in which they're launching this war is by claiming that whites hate everybody else...It's part of the strategy that Barack Obama implemented in 2008, continued in 2012, where he divides us all on race, on sex, greed, envy, class warfare, all those kinds of things. Well that's not true."

~ *Rep. Mo Brooks, (R) Alabama*

The power of privilege is the power to accuse the victims of the very crime being perpetrated upon them by the powerful.

And men and boys of color are being murdered to support the hatred and fear of the privileged.

A mother should not have to mourn the passing of her child when she should have been celebrating his first day of college. She should not be bequeathed her son's murder as a symbol of racism. Why should she have to shoulder that burden? My heart breaks for Lezley McSpadden and all the others who lost loved ones this way. Why and how is this happening today in this country?

We are a racially divided country, where groups are segregated by skin color and do not receive equal protection under the law. In fact, the law targets people of color through profiling, confrontational stops and frisks, which Trump promised to go back to even though the practice was ruled unconstitutional, and harsher sentencing by the judicial system. President Trump's Muslim ban, his stance on undocumented immigrants, and his claim that he is the law-and-order president, further segregate and target those who are not white and Christian.

Privilege leads one to believe the police and judicial system are there for you and your kind only, sworn to serve and protect you, while pursuing others. Even if you end up on the wrong side of the law, you are innocent until proven guilty by a jury of your peers.

Privilege is not just wealth. Most people don't aspire to great wealth, and only one percent of Americans can call themselves wealthy. Privilege is about feeling safe in your skin and being yourself: living, working, playing, and worshipping where and how you choose; and feeling validated every day and every hour of your life as you negotiate your way in society.

It's privilege when one believes his way and his people are better and more deserving and more right than others. It's privilege that makes one believe others are less than and deserve to be controlled and contained. It may appear to be invisible but there it is, wrapping around you, protecting you, giving you confidence, making you proud, and making you believe that the murder of black men and boys is either justified, or it is someone else's problem.

Many white Americans deny their role and complicity in systemic racism and the privilege they enjoy as white Americans. That's part of the privilege, too, the ability to deny and distance oneself or to just choose silence. They will feel anger as they read this or hear people talking about racism.

Victims and the people disenfranchised by white privilege are not in the position to change this dynamic. Those who willfully support racism, segregation, and white supremacy certainly will not act to change it. Only those, like me, who benefit directly from privilege, yet understand how unfair such an advantage is, can change the way privilege operates in our society.

If you are ethnically white and you do not support a racist society, acknowledge that not everyone experiences life in America as you do. Believe that every single American has a right to the kind of life only a sector of Americans, white Americans, exclusively enjoys now, and let that thinking be your guide and your conscience. The alternative is to acknowledge that you support inequality, and, like many Trump supporters, choose white supremacy as the system that operates behind the scenes in our country.

Put up your hands in protest. Vote in protest. Congregate in protest. Take a knee during the anthem in protest. Resist. Persist. Stand for equality, inclusiveness, and solidarity. Speak out against privilege, segregation, and injustice. Do it peaceably, because a violent response to violence only makes it worse, and gives the powerful and the privileged more power and privilege.

I know we can be better. We proved it in the days after Trump's election, when millions congregated in protest. We proved it after racist Nazis descended on Charlottesville, Virginia, armed with weapons and hatred, and one of them killed Heather Heyer, a white woman, and injured nineteen others, while several others chased and beat Deandre Harris, a black man, with metal flag poles. We can declare all the people of America equal, with an equal voice and an equal vote, all welcome to enjoy equal protection under the law, the right to exercise our freedoms in safety, and to know that those who are sworn to serve and protect us will do so in our time of need.

My heart is broken, but my spirit tells me, even now, in the clutches of a Trump presidency, that we have to keep trying.

Chapter 13
This is What Apartheid Looks Like in America

Words failed me after the grand jury determined on November 24, 2014, that no charges would be filed against Darren Wilson, the police officer who shot and killed Michael Brown. America failed in race relations again.

I spent a sleepless night after Prosecutor Robert McColloch spent half an hour defending the grand jury process, even though his use of it was far outside standard. He spent most of that time bashing witnesses' credibility and Michael Brown's character and defending Darren Wilson, the man against whom he was supposed to be considering charges. With nine whites and three blacks on the jury, no other outcome was possible. I knew this, even while holding onto a glimmer of hope. Six months later, the Department of Justice would report there was not enough reliable evidence to pursue a case against Wilson.

As soon as McColloch finished his announcement, I watched the streets of Ferguson swirl into chaos, fire, anguish, rage, and hopelessness.

This is what apartheid looks like in America. This is the systemic implementation of racist and biased policies, laws, and actions in our courtrooms, in our neighborhoods, in stand-your-ground laws that seem expressly written for the protection of white Americans, and in the ethnic and racial makeup of a militarized police presence.

CNN reported, "Wilson called the area where Brown was shot a 'hostile environment.'"

Wilson testified, "There's a lot of gangs that reside or associate with that area. There's a lot of violence in that area, there's a lot of gun activity, drug activity. It is just not a very well-liked community. That community doesn't like the police."

Why would this community possibly be suspicious of police? The police and the city used the community as a source of income, issuing tickets and fining people based on petty charges. The police presence was not positive, but a force of containment and oppression.

I believe it is a high-crime area. There is a lot of poverty with few paths out. That causes an environment where some believe crime is acceptable. But not all citizens who live there believe that, and they live good, honest lives. They should be afforded the same police protections that the rest of America, white America, enjoys. They are there by circumstance, not necessarily by choice. Why do the police, officials, and the media impugn the whole community, and not just the criminals? How can a police officer adequately protect and serve a community he doesn't like?

He can't.

Justice is bankrupt, and racism prevails.

While we argue causes and fling hatred and suspicion back and forth, more black men and boys die.

Including Tamir Rice, a twelve-year-old carrying a toy gun, in Cleveland, Ohio. Did you look at his face? He was a child. How did all the adults in this situation get everything so wrong? Racial bias blinded them.

New information on this case was released in 2017. The man who called 911 said Tamir was "probably a juvenile" and the gun he had was "probably fake." Constance Hollinger, who took the call, violated protocol when she failed to communicate that crucial information to the dispatcher, who then led police to believe Tamir was an adult male with a real gun. Hollinger, who was also disciplined in 2016 "for treating a 12-year-old girl who was reporting that she was sexually assaulted in a 'rude and unprofessional manner,'" was suspended for just eight days, which Samaria Rice, Tamir's mother, called "unacceptable." I agree.

Hollinger has since resigned. Sadly, this new information does not disprove the role racial bias had in Tamir's murder, but it proves conclusively that failing to adhere to protocol can be deadly as well.

In addition, both police officers faced internal disciplinary measures in May 2017 after a two-year investigation. No charges were filed by the grand jury, held in December 2015. Officer Garmback was suspended for pulling the police car up too close to Tamir. Officer Loehmann was fired for failing to disclose on his application that he was fired during probation from the Independence, Ohio police department for "emotional instability, disregard for training, and ineptitude." Unfortunately, the Cleveland police department never checked his employment record. Samaria Rice said the department's disciplinary actions were "deeply disappointing."

No justice was served for Tamir Rice and his family.

Ronald left the house twenty minutes before the verdict of the Darren Wilson case was read. We had already watched four hours of coverage, and he said he didn't want to see the verdict. He did not want to relive the George Zimmerman verdict. We had watched that verdict together. I cried; he got angry, then silent.

I knew I had to watch, even as I understood he could not. I kissed him goodbye and told him to be careful. He already knew the verdict, and my silence when he got home, and again the next morning, confirmed it.

I understand hopelessness. I saw it in the faces of the protesters, in the tears shed by Michael Brown's family, in the comments on my Facebook page, and in the way Ronald grows more introspective daily. I suffer the same hopelessness.

If we don't fight for change, the violence will grow and more black boys and men will die, not just physically, but emotionally and mentally. The death of black men and boys is an epidemic in this country.

I also understand that the election of a mixed-race president did not usher us into a post-racial world. Instead, it brought to light the very real inequality and injustice under which our society operates. President Obama's term created an incredible pushback in the election of President Trump, who ran with open supremacist support. Denial won't change or erase these events, which document the power of racism.

The things that will change systemic racism in law enforcement are the following:

1. Video cameras on every police officer and on every dashboard that must be operational at all stops;

2. Police departments that reflect the racial and ethnic makeup of the communities they serve;

3. Community policing instead of an adversarial, militarized police presence;

4. De-escalation training;

5. Testing to determine if a candidate for a position in law enforcement demonstrates racial bias and to determine how an individual responds under conditions of extreme stress;

6. Access to counseling and other mental health resources for officers;

7. Deconstructing the blue wall of silence so that officers can safely report, without threat of retaliation, colleagues who engage in conduct unbecoming a police officer, including excessive use of force;

8. Disciplinary action, including termination, when officers engage in profiling and/or excessive use of force;

9. Viable citizen review boards;

10. Better and more comprehensive diversity training for officers;

11. No hiring of officers who lost their positions at other police departments due to emotional instability, racial bias, or excessive use of force;

12. No employing of ticket quotas, stop-and-frisk quotas, or fine revenue quotas;

13. Enforcing equality in the criminal justice system including the charges brought against offenders, sentencing, and the length of prison terms.

We also need to have that conversation about race in America.

Let me be brutally honest: If you believe race does not affect your life, then you are one of the privileged in this country. If you don't care about or support the growing use of unnecessary force against citizens of color, you are racist and one of the privileged. If you don't care about black boys and men being killed at the hands of police officers, vigilantes hiding behind stand-your-ground laws, and white supremacist terrorists, you are a racist and one of the privileged. If you believe that every black community is full of lazy and lawless people, you are a racist and one of the privileged.

This is a tragedy for all Americans, not just black Americans.

We need to dig down into the history of our country and the institutional and systemic factors that cause bias and oppression. We need to acknowledge how this country was taken from the indigenous peoples and how it was built on the backs of slaves. We need to acknowledge that we continue to create an underclass through subpoverty wages, substandard schools, inaccessibility to healthcare, the creation of poor communities that lack access to healthy, affordable food and public transportation (food deserts), and the high cost of college tuition and high-interest student loans.

We need to educate the public about these truths and enact laws that protect equality. Federal oversight is needed, because we already know that states fail to achieve equality and justice for their citizens. Ferguson has proven the need for federal oversight with the appointment of a biased prosecutor, an almost all-white police force in a city that is 70 percent black, a jury that was predominately white, and in the militarized response to legitimate protests.

The advocacy group Black Lives Matter organized many protests in Ferguson, and other cities across the country. Started by three black women in response to Trayvon Martin's murder, the group trains protesters in peaceful demonstration techniques, advocates for equality, and hosts other events to educate America about the racism that rages in our country. In its words: "#BlackLivesMatter is working for a world where Black lives are no longer systematically and intentionally targeted for demise. We affirm our contributions to this society, our humanity, and our resilience in the face of deadly oppression. We have put our sweat equity and love for Black people into creating a political project—taking the hashtag off of social media and into the streets. The call for Black lives to matter is a rallying cry for ALL Black lives striving for liberation." Unfortunately, during the protests in Ferguson, the media concentrated its coverage on the rioters who damaged property, instead of the thousands who protested peacefully. In much the same way that the men and boys who are murdered die a second time through character assassination by the far-right media such as *Breitbart* and *InfoWars*, Black Lives Matter has been vilified as being a racist, militant, and violent organization. Once again, the backlash is twice the progress made.

If we don't make changes immediately, black men and boys will continue to die in record numbers.

This is what apartheid looks like in America.

Chapter 14
Long, Cold Winter of Justice

"How long? Not long, because the arc of the moral universe is long, but it bends toward justice."
~ *Dr. Martin Luther King, Jr.*

Cold temperatures drive me inside my head. I lived in upstate New York for my first fifty years, but I never liked the cold. At best I could tolerate it, swearing or crying into my muffler as I pushed snow off my car, or straining against the wind to get to my building's door each morning for work, hoping the wind would not knock me off my feet, as it had on other occasions.

When Ronald bought me a remote car starter, my mood lightened. I could open the door of my building, aim the remote at the car in the parking lot twenty-five yards away, and start my car. Twenty minutes later, I would brave the wind and chill and jump into my warm car. I didn't even have to scrape windows.

Down South, I complain if I have to put on socks. The winter of 2014–2015 was one of the coldest I remember since moving here, and it made me want to hibernate. Up north, we would have been cheering at how mild a winter it was.

Sometimes Ronald says we should move farther south to Florida, and I just stare at him blankly. Another state with bad politics, only Florida doesn't have the grand topography or the same brilliant blue sky of North Carolina, and there are too many people.

The chill made me think of my writing life, too. It had been harshly vacant, like one of my mornings up north, walking to my building, the cold piercing and the wind pushing.

I had reasons or excuses. The world was overwhelming

and too many bad things were happening, like a terrorist bombing in Paris, or the murder of a young black man at the hands of the police.

Sometimes, I wanted to shut down the newsfeeds and recycle the paper before reading it.

It happened with family, too. All the years of estrangement, the legacy of it carried from one generation to the next, the sameness in its execution, like it's genetic. One day I stopped thinking about it, and then, I stopped thinking about them.

Our history seems genetically coded, too. Violence, oppression, hatred, distrust, greed, and racial bias—they are passed on, the same as hair color and texture, eye color, height, body type, and skin color.

Greed and self-centeredness make us poor stewards of the earth and poor advocates of the greater good. President Trump proved that when he pulled our country out of the Paris climate accord.

I am as guilty as anyone these days, with my armchair activism. I write and post my opinions on Facebook, but you won't find me out marching anymore. There was a time I spoke up, lobbied, and protested. I made the effort to make effective change in my workplace, at my daughters' school, in my community, and at the state and national level.

My generation knew we had to do something to make change back then. We knew we had to voice our concerns, not in a room filled with like minds, but in the room of minds least likely to agree.

When Ronald and I went to see *Selma* in 2015, I was reminded why we felt that way. I would turn eight just a couple of months after the marches from Selma to Montgomery. I remember watching the news about it, but I don't ever remember discussing it in school. Even though it would change our history, it apparently did not affect us in my mostly white school up north, where I never shared a classroom with any of the few black students in my school district, and where I cannot recall a single black teacher.

Something in me knew that omission was wrong. Somehow, I knew this was important, even though it would be years before I understood racial bias and just how insidious and pervasive institutional and systemic racism is in our country.

But something else happened, too. Organizations like the Southern Christian Leadership Conference (SCLC), the Student Nonviolent Coordinating Committee (SNCC), and the Congress of Racial Equality (CORE) taught the country about the necessity of protest to make change.

Here's a quote from Dr. King's speech delivered in Montgomery after the march:

If it may be said of the slavery era that the white man took the world and gave the Negro Jesus, then it may be said of the Reconstruction era that the southern aristocracy took the world and gave the poor white man Jim Crow. (Yes, sir.) He gave him Jim Crow. (Uh huh.) And when his wrinkled stomach cried out for the food that his empty pockets could not provide, (Yes, sir,) he ate Jim Crow, a psychological bird that told him that no matter how bad off he was, at least he was a white man, better than the black man. (Right sir.) And he ate Jim Crow. (Uh huh.) And when his undernourished children cried out for the necessities that his low wages could not provide, he showed them the Jim Crow signs on the buses and in the stores, on the streets and in the public buildings. (Yes, sir.) And his children, too, learned to feed upon Jim Crow, (Speak.) their last outpost of psychological oblivion. (Yes, sir.)

I still feel the relevance of this speech. The lie of superiority is still being peddled.

Before we even arrived at the theater, I could feel my emotions thrumming. Ronald was unsure he wanted to see it. As he has often said, "I live this."

"I want to see it as an adult," I countered.

He relented. I feel guilty that he must share my journey to understand racism, when he already has an intimate knowledge of it. After forty years, I cannot say that I know what it is like to be black in America. White Americans may think I'm daft, but black Americans know what I mean.

At the theater, there were very few white people in the audience. Why didn't they come to learn about our collective history?

I knew Addie Mae Collins, Cynthia Wesley, Carole Robertson, and Denise McNair would die in the stairwell of the 16th Street Baptist Church in Birmingham, Alabama, but I leaped and gasped aloud when the blast decimated those innocent souls, who each had all the potential in the world, but no chance to reach it.

When Jimmie Lee Jackson, church deacon and civil rights activist, was gunned down by a police officer during a nonviolent protest, I began to cry.

I cried all the way through the movie credits.

I cried for the valor displayed by people who knew they might die, but showed up anyway. I cried for the injustices perpetrated by the very people who are supposed to protect and serve us, the peace officers, who chose instead to uphold Jim Crow. I cried because I understood the symbolism of the Confederate flag. I cried because what happened then is not so different from what is happening now. I cried because this was a story that we all share, told finally from the perspective of the people oppressed by Jim Crow.

In 1965, the police galloped into the marchers on horses and wielded bats and tear gas. In Ferguson, they arrived in tanks, wore riot gear, and used rubber bullets and tear gas.

Today, protests are mostly done from inside the comfort of one's home on social media, where most friends agree. Though I am guilty of it, I don't think it changes a single thing. When people do take to the streets, they often are not organized, as they were during the Civil Rights marches. Dr. King and those close advisors and collaborators around him had direction, concrete demands, and strategies. The protesters were trained and understood what to expect. (Black Lives Matter trained many protesters in Ferguson in this tradition). Little was left to chance.

Today someone tweets to meet up at Times Square, and thousands show up, but what is the plan, what are the demands, what are the strategies?

While we are quick to gather in the streets and lament and commiserate on social media, others are working hard to implement their agendas of privilege and power. Since the election of President Trump, protests have become better organized, participant numbers are astounding, and the protests have contributed to stopping executive orders and the passage of discriminatory laws, such as the Muslim ban executive order and the GOP repeal and replace of the Affordable Care Act, but we still have more to do.

It scares me when I think about how we have regressed in race relations in our country. Hate crimes increased under the Trump administration. White supremacists are grateful to Trump for bringing their rhetoric into mainstream consciousness. What I wonder is what I could have done differently, what my generation could have done differently. I hope the younger generations figure it out. Black Lives Matter gives me hope.

I think we've failed as liberals and activists in the last fifty years.

Part of our failure was the complacency that comes from success. When we believed we had achieved all we set out to do, we stopped being vigilant, and Jim Crow gained ground again.

The other part of failure is that white liberals still live

with privilege and still view the world through the lens of privilege.

I watched Chris Matthews discuss *Selma* in a segment on his show *Hardball*. I have great respect for this man, but I watched him get prickly because he didn't feel President Johnson was respectfully and truthfully portrayed in the film. His reaction to the film says to me that white liberals want to be liberal, but keep the old order.

They still like to be the ones in control, the power brokers, and the ones in the know. It is damaging in the quest for racial equality. As soon as a white liberal tells a person of color "I get it," or "You don't understand what needs to be done," he or she is being patronizing and racist.

When a white person says, "I get it," it is like telling Samaria Rice you know how she felt when Tamir was gunned down by a police officer less than two seconds after the officers pulled up to him while he played with a toy gun in the park. Fuck, no, we don't know.

When Chris Matthews lamented about LBJ's reputation, he stole the story from black Americans who were tired of oppression and ready to demand change and gave it to a "white savior," who swept in to save the day for the poor black fools who couldn't save themselves without his assistance. I know that's not what he meant, but the narrative was there, just beneath the surface.

That's not the story Ava Duvernay chose to tell, nor was it the truth or the story we needed to hear. Certainly, LBJ was a wealthy white man with a Southern affiliation, and he was blatant in his use of the N-word. He enacted both the Civil Rights Act and the Voting Rights Act, but it is doubtful he would have acted alone. He did what was right politically and right for the country, and there is no doubt his decision to act was in direct reaction to Dr. King's persuasiveness and the powerful microscope of the news media focused on the

South.

I've had family and friends alike tell Ronald they get it, or, they tell him that the experience he is relating couldn't possibly have happened. His story made them uncomfortable, and their privilege ephemeral, and instead of expressing those feelings, they attacked his credibility. I've stopped talking to family members and friends, or they've stopped talking to me. I've been unfriended on Facebook because so-called friends did not want to allow that my experience is different from theirs. Estrangement is the easy way out for both of us. The other person doesn't have to endure uncomfortable moments, and I don't have to feel offended by their inability to accept a different experience.

We, who look at the world from the safe haven of privilege, cannot ever know what it is to be unprivileged and targeted in America. Part of the privilege is the assuredness often displayed when telling people who are not privileged that you know more about their lives than they do.

Even though I gave up whiteness when I entered into an interracial relationship over forty years ago, I am not black. I cannot know what my husband and daughters experience as black and mixed-race Americans. What I relate here are my narratives, not theirs, even when they star in them.

I regain my white status in the eyes of others as soon as I am alone.

What I can do is demonstrate my outrage at the perpetrators of racism, give an empathetic ear when things happen, speak up when it matters, and continue my journey to learn about race in America and my role in perpetuating racism. Forty years is not long enough, because it's already been proven that fifty years, or even 150 years, cannot undo our history.

That is what we, the people defined as white in our racially constructed society, need to do. Listen. Acknowledge privilege. Speak up, instead of choosing silence. Express outrage. Collaborate to work toward a solution.

Are we capable of accepting another societal construct, one that eliminates racial divides and gives every citizen equal opportunity and equality under the law?

Can we change our inherent need for tribalism by redefining our tribes?

Can we agree that equality is more desirable than privilege, which assumes a construct of haves and have-nots?

I need a remote starter to defrost my heart, because I don't trust we can achieve this.

Aside from watching *Selma*, two moments that week reminded me not to give up hope.

Ronald turned to me as we were driving home one night and said, "Your looks change, and today you look like that photo I took of you on my parents' porch."

I knew the one he meant, taken one warm, spring day in college. "In my sleeveless sweater," I said.

The photo was taken in 1977, a time when my parents, particularly my mother, railed against my relationship with Ronald. In one argument that summer, she would accuse me of causing my father's second heart attack. It was also when Ronald and I knew we would spend our lives together, because neither of us could imagine a different future.

The second was on that Saturday morning. After writing for a bit, I climbed back into bed and shaped my body around Ronald's contours. Our combined body heat was tropical. Soon we turned in unison, and, lying side-by-side, his left hand holding my right hand above our heads, we talked about everything and nothing. It was the most meaningful hour of my day.

Those moments are my remote starter. They warm me up and keep me going, no matter how cold it gets.

Chapter 15
Sleeting Justice

In February 2015, as the cold weather continued to stymie me, I wondered, "What I should write about?" The father who killed his transgender child? The Christian woman who beat her Jewish friend in an effort to convert her? The atheist who murdered his Muslim neighbors because he didn't like where they parked?

Instead I chose to write about my own neighbor, the one who discharged her firearm through her overhead garage door at people she did not see. Another neighbor said she told her that she "heard Mexican voices" and just shot. When I contacted the police by e-mail, since I was the homeowners' association president by that time, the officer said the report on the gunfire was confidential because a small child was involved. He also said the garage door was pried up in the corner, (Really? That's quite hard to visualize and must have taken some work and time, and the other neighbor said she couldn't see where the door had been pried), and since she was home alone with a small child, my shooter neighbor had a right to fire her weapon. What happened to leaving the garage, going back in the house, and locking the door, while dialing 911? How about calling out, "I have a gun. I'm on the phone with 911. Leave my property now!"

A few weeks later, she was on our HOA Google group complaining about a new resident in the neighborhood who had not even lived in his house a week. Would she shoot him because she didn't like the sound of his truck?

I didn't know if the new neighbors were Muslims, but I knew they were black. Almost all her complaints were about black or Hispanic men or boys. She had logged thirty-three calls to the police in five years. The officer did not think that was excessive.

That doesn't count the times she complained or bragged on the Google group. I sent all of those to the police officer, too, and he said not all the dates matched up to a police report, meaning, there were many instances where she reported an incident or suspicious person to our Google group, but never reported it to the police.

She's the same person I wrote about in chapter three of this book. She described the intruder from that incident as having "evil eyes." She also admitted she may have left her door unlocked.

Just like she left her SUV parked on the street with her purse in the front seat. The vehicle doors were unlocked then, too.

If the temperature is above fifty, which is most days of the year down here, when we lived in that neighborhood, I would leave the door open. I loved the extra light it let in. We picked that house because of all the oversized windows. I love a light-filled home. The difference? We had a security glass door. It locked with two huge hook bolts that fit into slots in steel-reinforced timber. The glass was bulletproof. An elephant might be able to knock it down, but I never saw any of those in the neighborhood. We also owned a dog and a security system, and there was a wrought iron gate on our porch—you'd be surprised how many people couldn't figure out how to open it. We had motion lights and the yard was open all around the house, no privacy fences or hedges.

We aren't paranoid, but we understand when the police tell you to make your house an unattractive target.

It's not that there was a lot of crime in our neighborhood. Including the neighbor who called the police thirty-three times in five years, (which averages out to 6.6 calls per year), we averaged 7.8 break-in/property damage calls per year in the same period, 2009–2014. There were seventy-eight homes in the neighborhood. Suffice it to say that most of the calls were hers.

I called the police four times in the ten years we lived there: twice when my car was hit in the driveway, (we lived on a curve, and after the city installed a sign letting people know there was a curve up ahead, it didn't happen again); the third time was when a rabid coyote was rolling around on the front lawn; and the fourth time was when the house next door to us was in foreclosure and I saw two white guys come out carrying the heat pump and loading it into the back of their pickup.

I knew the two white men were not the owners, because I knew the prior owners. I suspected they were members of the original construction crew, because that heat pump was well-hidden in an attic crawlspace inside a closet.

We lived in the city. There will be crime. That's what happens when a lot of people live fairly close together. The economy down here was terrible, too, and the state government had removed or shortened the term of just about every safety net. Some people will turn to crime out of desperation, and some will turn to crime because they are bad people.

But city living is a choice. I prefer the city. There is more going on, more people to run into, services like trash collection are better, and the fire departments are full-time, not volunteer.

Living out in the country is a choice, too, and, like the officer told us when we invited him to speak at our HOA meeting, people choose that option because they don't want to be around people. Why didn't my neighbor move? She kept talking about it, as in this post on the neighborhood Google group, complaining about the new neighbor's truck, "I mean I was ready to pack up and go yesterday over break-ins but this unnecessary noise has got to stop!"

Ronald responded out loud to her post, "Then go, already."

He was ready to go over to the new neighbor and warn him. I e-mailed and warned his landlord instead. I didn't want Ronald walking near that woman's house, but he did, anyway, when things continued to escalate because he was concerned someone would get hurt. I didn't want to read in the paper that the new neighbor was shot and killed because the shooter neighbor thought his truck was loud because she could hear his music as he pulled into the driveway. It reminded me too much of the atheist in Durham, North Carolina, who didn't like where his Muslim neighbors parked, so he shot and killed them. When did that become a reason to kill someone?

When did we become so paranoid that the pried edge of a garage door justifies blasting a hole in the door in front of your own child and in a residential city neighborhood?

The officer to whom I sent my email with the shooter neighbor's many posts of suspicious people and break-ins reminded me of our Second Amendment rights. He said I was judgmental, and my statements were inflammatory.

Protect and serve. I was glad my shooter neighbor, whose husband was a deputy in another county, was getting the full benefit of the city police service, while the rest of us worried about our right to walk and drive our neighborhood streets and live in our homes safely.

I reserved my right to wonder if that garage door was truly pried at the corner, or if what the other neighbor related was really the truth: that the shooter neighbor didn't see the door pried up, "heard Mexican voices," never laid eyes on anyone, and shot blindly through the door. One of the NRA rules of gun safety is as follows, and I went to the experts: Know your target and what is beyond.

That summer she was at it again. By that time, we were monitoring her e-mails and not allowing them to post on the

Google group. Just hours before an HOA meeting, she e-mailed about the police capturing an escaped prisoner behind her house. She said, "Why does this stuff always happen to me?" She claimed to have seen him on the main road outside our neighborhood, then again on her porch. She said she recognized his dreadlocks and knew he was the prisoner, but he had left her porch before she had a chance to retrieve her Glock, and then the police got him—behind her house. We did not post her e-mail. There was an escaped prisoner and he was caught that evening, but it wasn't behind her house. It was six miles away.

At the HOA meeting that I was facilitating as president, while waiting a few more minutes for neighbors to wander in and get seated, I congratulated the guest officer on the capture. He was the same officer who had told me I was being judgmental and inflammatory about my shooter neighbor, but that evening he was chatty and friendly, willing to talk about the capture. The capture only took a couple of days, unlike the hunt up in New York state that happened at the same time. That one took authorities three weeks to find the two prisoners who, just like the North Carolina case, were aided in their escape by a prison guard. The officer at the meeting looked proud and said it was easy, because they knew he'd go back to his girlfriend. I asked him how far the arrest was made from our neighborhood, and he told me about six miles. He didn't know about the e-mail that we didn't post to our Google group, and I didn't tell him about it—not yet, anyway.

Later in the meeting when neighbors were encouraged to ask questions of the officer about safety, several neighbors brought up the shooting through the garage door, again, because I wasn't the only neighbor upset about it. The officer went through his Second Amendment Rights speech and said that, no matter what, he would stand by her right to protect herself and her child, even if she never laid eyes on anyone. Ronald got up and explained how dangerous it was for neighbors of color in the neighborhood, since she was always reporting that every black person she saw was suspicious. He related the story about the police officer who demanded Ronald's driver's license to prove he lived at our house when the police saw him working on the yard. He quoted the police officer swearing at him when he asked for his license, an aggressive response to a man who had every right to rake his lawn. The pastor, who was also a neighbor, of the church where we were having the meeting kicked Ronald out for swearing in the house of the Lord. So, I thought, cursing, even if you are quoting someone else, is viler to this man than shooting a person of color just for the offense of having brown skin, or speaking a different language, or being someplace a white person thinks you don't belong.

Yet I wasn't surprised the pastor wanted to kick Ronald out of the church, because Ronald had whispered an incident in my ear that occurred just after we arrived. I had gone in ahead to make sure the room was set up for our meeting, while Ronald carried in the snacks I had purchased. As he entered the church, carrying gallon jugs of cider and a Dunkin Donuts box, a parishioner stopped him in the hallway and asked him why he was there, even though some of the other neighbors were starting to wander in at the same time. The parishioner must have been startled to see a black man in her church.

After Ronald left and the pastor locked the door so he couldn't come back in, I stood for effect and told the police officer and the neighbors that shooter neighbor had claimed the prisoner was caught behind her house. The neighborhood watch leader verified it. The officer was quiet, his chatty camaraderie gone.

At the close of the meeting, I approached the pastor to tell him that Ronald quoted the police officer so people would know how quickly such a stop could escalate, but that he doesn't normally swear. The pastor kept his back to me as he turned the thermostat down and said nothing.

I asked the only other black neighbors in the room, a couple, if they could give me a ride home. I did not feel enough trust to ask any of the white neighbors. When we got outside, Ronald was sitting in our car waiting for me. On the way home he told me that when the police officer came out of the building after the meeting, Ronald approached him and further explained why the shooter neighbor made our neighborhood a dangerous place. "He knows I'm right," he said.

My shooter neighbor didn't try to e-mail the Google group after that evening, and I wondered if the officer had paid her a visit. It was odd she stopped so suddenly, and his silence when I told him about the shooter neighbor's email, and then Ronald's additional talk with him outside the meeting, made me think he finally understood how dangerous this neighbor could be to the rest of us, a neighbor with a gun who made up dramatic stories so she had an excuse to discharge it. She is not unlike many who own guns and hope to find a situation in which to use them. George Zimmerman, Michael Dunn, and John Henry Spooner come to mind.

Later, after I resigned as president of the HOA, her e-mails began appearing on the Google group again.

I remember hoping, when I started seeing her messages again, that I would never read about her in the paper.

Chapter 16
No More

I grew angry in 2015 as the year wore on. I'd been speaking out and fighting for equality, fairness, and justice my entire adult life, and the years since President Obama won the 2008 election had been some of the most difficult. Millions of others, including those who must fight every day of their lives for equal treatment, must have shared my anger, frustration, and disappointment.

But there are still millions who think racism, sexism, or gender rights don't have anything to do with them. They are the ones who voted for Trump. There are others who wage a war of hatred, violence, and terrorism, often based on their religious or white supremacist beliefs, which they claim others are violating or trying to hamper.

The intersection of these different perspectives is causing us fits. Worse, it is endangering certain people, impacting their social and economic standing in our country, and killing them.

The Charleston massacre, executed on June 17, 2015, by a cowardly racist, was just another in a long list of violent acts perpetrated in our country. Lots of pundits wanted to call terrorist Dylann Roof a lone wolf who suffered some sort of mental illness, but he was ruled competent to stand trial. Others went straight to calling it an attack on religious freedom—really, the irony only made me angrier. The very people crying their religious freedom was being attacked were the same people who helped groom terrorists like Roof.

The truth is we caused this massacre. We caused it through our complacency, our denial, and our refusal as a nation to recognize that inequality exists because it is engineered into our societal, institutional, and systemic structures. We live in a racist country. The majority of

Americans, white people, are racist, because they directly benefit socially and economically. Individuals may not recognize, acknowledge, or feel privileged, as some white Americans live in poverty with few options, but it is there, nonetheless, more visible the higher one climbs the economic ladder. Individuals may feel they are not racist and may even support equality, but the system is designed to privilege them, while it is detrimental to people of color. If we don't have this conversation, in an honest and open way, this will go on and on, as it has for hundreds of years.

Worse are the states that live in hypocrisy. Right after the Charleston massacre, some, including South Carolina, removed the stars and bars from their capitols and from their license plates, while others took down monuments dedicated to men who committed treason by fighting on the side of the Confederacy. Many of these monuments were erected during the height of the Jim Crow era to intimidate people of color and remind them their freedoms were limited. These steps to correct our history are very important, but shallow if we do not acknowledge that much more must be done, including disavowing racism in our past and in the present, and teaching the real history of our country, not the one pushed by white supremacists.

Even the GOP backed away from support of the Confederate flag. At first, South Carolina Senator Lindsey Graham said in defense of the Confederate flag flown on state grounds, "It is a part of who we are." A day later, he stood next to Governor Nikki Haley as she announced there would be discussion to have it removed, and the flag was removed on July 10, 2015.

New Orleans removed its Confederate monuments in May 2017, "which critics deemed symbols of racism and intolerance and which supporters viewed as historically important." Workers were dressed to conceal their identities for protection, and the removals were not announced in advance and were scheduled at night to minimize conflict. Mayor Landrieu said, "The removal of these statues sends a clear and unequivocal message to the people of New Orleans and the nation: New Orleans celebrates our diversity, inclusion and tolerance. This is not about politics, blame or retaliation. This is not a naïve quest to solve all our problems at once. This is about showing the whole world that we as a city and as a people are able to acknowledge, understand, reconcile — and most importantly — choose a better future." While other cities followed suit, including Baltimore, MD, some cities and states held fast to leaving the monuments right where they are by voting in legislative protections.

On August 12, 2017, white supremacists marched at a rally called Unite the Right, in support of saving a monument of Robert E. Lee from being removed in Charlottesville, Virginia. They came armed with bats and rifles and incited violence. One of them ran his car into a crowd of counter-protesters, striking and killing Heather Heyer and injuring nineteen others. Reminiscent of a scene from the 1967 movie *In the Heat of the Night*, starring Sidney Poitier, Deandre Harris was beaten with poles by a gang of supremacists who chased him into a parking garage. While Poitier's character Virgil Tibbs came out of the incident unscathed in the movie, Deandre Harris suffered debilitating injuries including a spinal injury and a head laceration that required eight staples. Former Governor Terry McAuliffe called for the arrest and prosecution of the perpetrators, and four were identified and arrested.

But another warrant for arrest was issued after the attack, in October 2017—calling for the arrest of Deandre Harris, who is still recovering from his injuries and who now suffers anxiety in public spaces. This warrant was not issued by the Charlottesville police department that had promised to investigate the original complaint, but by the city magistrate. The police were surprised.

Deandre's attorney S. Lee Merritt said that as one of the white supremacists was trying to spear another counter-protester with the sharp end of his flagpole, right before the gang of supremacists beat Deandre unconscious, Deandre tried to stop the supremacist by swinging at the flagpole with a flashlight, but he "failed to make significant contact." The supremacist claimed Deandre caused injuries that "permanently scarred" him. Merritt contends the supremacist's injuries were actually sustained later in the day, after Deandre had already been transported to the emergency room at the Sentara Martha Jefferson Hospital. Video shows a white man, dressed in black, bashing the supremacist with what looks like a metal pipe.

Merritt was convinced this legal attack on Deandre "is, in my opinion, clearly an exploitation of the criminal justice system. The person who is the complainant in the case is an attorney and it feels like he used some of his lawyer friends to manufacture some of these charges that never should have gone forward."

Brad Griffin, spokesman for the League of the South, one of the groups who organized the rally, and the organization in which the supremacist attorney is a state leader, said that a group including Deandre Harris started the fray that ended in the parking garage. He claimed the attorney's flagpole was grabbed by one of the counter-protesters, who proceeded to spin the attorney around. He alleged Deandre Harris took that opportunity to hit the attorney on the left side of his face, and this caused the brawl where Deandre was beaten unconscious just yards from the police station.

Yes, the supremacist who was carrying a Confederate flag—Harold Crews, who claims Deandre Harris hit him—is an attorney. He is the attorney who is the North Carolina state chapter chairman of the League of the South.

And he is the same attorney who provided legal services to my homeowners' association in my old neighborhood. He is the attorney my HOA chose to keep as legal counsel, while accepting my resignation from the board. He might even be one of the "fine people" President Trump referred to in his rant on Charlottesville.

Just days before the rally, the Southern Poverty Law Center released an article that profiled all the LOS state chapter chairmen. Crews was listed, and his profile said, aside from being the North Carolina chapter chairman, he "operates the League's Facebook, website and a podcast titled 'Southern Nationalist Radio,' where he frequently interviews Michael Hill [president and founder of the LOS], Mark Thomey of the Alabama League of the South, and Brad Griffin." He also videotapes the LOS annual meetings, including the 2017 meeting where celebrity white supremacist David Duke was a guest speaker. He is a member of the Sons of Confederate Veterans, a group other LOS members often describe as the "'weak sister' who cannot stand to be called a racist, anti-Semite, xenophobe, white supremacist."

Ronald heard me laughing in disbelief as I read about this in our local paper. I could summon no other emotion. The world just felt claustrophobic and absurd. When I told him what I was reading, he asked, "Do you feel vindicated?"

"No," I said. "The neighbors probably still side with him."

Echoing those neighbors who questioned my credibility and said that I had gotten my information about Crews from "that liberal" Southern Poverty Law Center, Griffin also claimed the SPLC "[is] not a credible source," because, "they hate white people."

Michael Hill, president of the League of the South, posted a photograph of Crews with his injury on the LOS website. Crews' face is turned to the side so that his swollen cheek and temple are clearly displayed. He is holding a large Confederate flag that seems to frame him in an embrace as if he were a war hero. The meme, stolen from one about Senator Elizabeth Warren, says, "Nevertheless, he persisted." The short description claims Harris was charged with felony malicious wounding against Crews and that updates would be posted. There were no updates, including this news: Deandre Harris was found not guilty of assault in March 2018.

A local publication titled *Triad City Beat*, featured Crews in an article, "Meet Harold Ray Crews, the Main Street White Nationalist," in December 2017. The article describes the LOS as "one of the most virulently racist far-right organizations in the United States, promoting a subset of fascist ideology known as Southern nationalism that seeks a white homeland in the states that make up the former Confederacy."

Although Crews refused to comment for the article, saying, "I don't speak to the media under any circumstance. Do not contact me again," the article contained several of his apparently prolific tweets. One said, "I support same-race marriage," and another said, "If you favor illegal immigration/amnesty then you're a traitor and deserve everything that's coming to you."

Since the first board meeting after I discovered Crews' affiliation with the LOS, and where we discussed the future of our business relationship with him, I wondered if one of my fellow board members might have belonged to a hate group. Maybe it was the lesson he attempted to impart on Civil War history from the Southern white perspective, eerily the same as the one I had read on the LOS website. He said I did not understand Southern heritage, and I asked him if that included the heritage of my parents-in-law. He told me, "More people in the South than you imagine are members of groups like this."

That comment stuck with me, but it wasn't until he later claimed during an open meeting with the neighbors on the topic, with an odd fealty and reverence in his voice, that the attorney was "part of the HOA; one of us," that I realized this board member had never had a reason before this incident that called for him to meet with, speak with, or even email Crews. We had no legal business to conduct during the officer's tenure on the board, and he had moved into the neighborhood just a couple of months before volunteering to serve on the board, so he had never met the man. That made me think he must have known Crews through another channel that had nothing to do with our HOA. It occurred to me his statement about more Southern people being members of hate groups than I imagined was more like a self-disclosure than a generalization. No wonder his lesson on the Civil War and Southern heritage was verbatim what I'd already read on the LOS website.

As some Americans communicated distress over the removal of Confederate monuments and battle flags, claiming liberals were trying to erase their history and heritage, I felt besieged in this North Carolina town, where the LOS attorney lived, and where I saw letters from his brother on the readers' page of the local newspaper every once in a while, including this letter from September 2017:

DONALD CREWS, *Winston-Salem*

True Nazis

A historical fact is that the party of Hitler, the Nazi party, used intimidation, violence and anarchy in order to suppress opposition groups and keep them from expressing any position that opposed the Nazi party. Their racist attitude was displayed in such events as the "night of the crystal glass," when the real Jewish persecution began and violence against businesses resulted in massive looting. No First Amendment rights existed except for the Nazi position and terror tactics were commonplace against opposing parties. Eventually all parties except the Nazi ceased to exist and individual citizens were imprisoned if they opposed the Nazi political and amoral position.

In view of the recent violence in Virginia and California one must ask: Who are the real Nazis, the white nationalists or the radical liberal left?

At the open meeting with the neighbors, scheduled about eight months after I resigned, the board announced Crews had resigned and that they were also resigning because they had received an anonymous threat. One board member, the person who took my place, in talking about the threat, stared straight at Ronald, the only black man in the room, as he charged he would use the full extent of the law if he felt he or his wife were in danger. But Ronald is not the kind of person who makes an anonymous complaint—we had been perfectly open about our thoughts on Crews, and my resignation was the action chosen. Surely, the person who made the threat chose to remain anonymous. Further, no one seemed bothered that Crews had been called in by the board to counsel them when I requested a change of attorney. I had told them that he had no right to participate in the discussion, since we just paid him for legal services that could be terminated at any time by either party. He was not a neighbor. He was no more a part of the HOA than the man we paid to mow our common areas. They may have been concerned about the anonymous threat made to them, but did they care that Crews had the full LOS membership, estimated to be between 10,000 to 15,000 members, standing behind him, and he knew where we lived, that we are an interracial couple, and that I was behind the discovery of his affiliations?

At the close of the meeting some neighbors claimed they wanted to be good neighbors now that it was all over. But as we left the meeting we were met by more than a few neighbors who had the kind of look we have come to call the "Southern stare." It is a look we became familiar with since moving down here, the look that bores holes through you, the one of disgust and contempt, the one that says our relationship is abhorrent, or that we are offensive, or that we don't belong in the same public space occupied by the person staring at us. We stopped speaking to the neighbors.

Three months after that meeting we put our house, the one we bought as our retirement home, on the market. They didn't ask us to leave, but who wants to live in a neighborhood where many of the neighbors feel more comfortable with a white supremacist than they do with an aging, interracial couple, or in a neighborhood where every black or brown person, neighbor or not, is considered suspicious and may get shot? We asked ourselves, as we waited for the house to sell, where in America could we go and escape that kind of scrutiny. Where is it safe in America if you are not part of the white majority?

Many Southern states still believe in segregation and a system of haves and have-nots. We know brown citizens are considered inferior to white citizens. LGBTQ citizens have fewer rights than heterosexual citizens. Women have fewer rights than men. Voting records, laws including voter suppression efforts, and the denial of safety nets, like Medicaid expansion and unemployment insurance, are indicators of inequality.

The Confederate flag gives rise to people like the racist terrorist Dylann Roof because the state supports and embraces a racist, violent heritage and history that includes attacks on historic black churches by way of not always punishing the perpetrators of the crimes. The history of the

Mother Emanuel AME Church is fraught with violence, including being burned to the ground in the 1820s by white South Carolinians, who believed a slave rebellion was being organized inside. This is the church where Roof gunned down nine worshipers during a prayer fellowship. They welcomed him when he wandered into the church, and he sat with them in prayer and fellowship before announcing he "had" to kill them.

Other systemic beliefs also feed the extremists. Politicians and certain media outlets, like Fox News, use racial bias to promote their conservative agenda. The birther conspiracy is perhaps the most notorious effort at delegitimizing our first black president, Barack Obama, and President Trump was its most visible and vocal supporter. Trump also refused to disavow white supremacy on several occasions, when he had every opportunity to do so, including when he described the violence in Charlottesville as perpetrated "on many sides."

We are a hypocritical country. Our greatest published ideal is that we are all created equal. Yet what goes on in this country is not even close to the ideal. We live divided—though not in the way the conservatives would have us believe. The system divides us. It was created and sustained purposely to keep white men in power. The powerful prey on the ignorance of the uneducated to keep racism going. There is nothing like dividing the country and then having one group, members of the ruling majority, claim the others cause all the ills.

And what do people do when they are angry and feel justified in their anger, when they watch Fox News or read *Breitbart*, search supremacist websites, hear Trump shout about making America great again, and listen to their clergy, who buy into divine bestowal of supremacy? They strike back. No, Dylann Roof was not a lone wolf. He is the monster

South Carolina created, and there are more like him, including the HOA attorney Crews. They showed up in Charlottesville, Virginia, and, like Roof, they hope to start a race war.

Is racism still a problem in America? Yes, but it was never a problem for white people who choose to ignore it, downplay it, deny it, or blame the victims. It's easier that way, and it is a direct benefit of being privileged.

As racism continues to be newsworthy, many white people show what Robin DiAngelo termed "white fragility." She describes it this way:

For white people, their identities rest on the idea of racism as about good or bad people, about moral or immoral singular acts, and if we're good, moral people we can't be racist—we don't engage in those acts. This is one of the most effective adaptations of racism over time—that we can think of racism as only something that individuals either are or are not "doing."

In large part, white fragility—the defensiveness, the fear of conflict—is rooted in this good/bad binary. If you call someone out, they think to themselves, "What you just said was that I am a bad person, and that is intolerable to me." It's a deep challenge to the core of our identity as good, moral people.

Many white people cannot have a conversation about race without getting defensive or shutting down. They will claim, "I'm a good person. I'm a Christian. I am not racist, but..." and they let loose with a tirade about how black people have it so nice because they get everything for free, or it is all their fault that they are in the situation they find themselves in, whether that is living in poverty, or imprisonment, or being stopped by police, or being in low-paying jobs with no benefits, or living in inadequate housing with old paint that contains lead, or drinking water that contains lead, or studying in schools that are not at the standard of many predominately white, suburban schools, or at the barrel end of a gun held by a racially biased police officer, vigilante, or white supremacist terrorist. They don't even acknowledge the millions of middle and upper-class blacks, who still struggle with daily microaggressions and larger issues like driving while black (DWB), higher interest rates for loans compared to equivalent white applicants, and workplace acceptance.

There are white individuals and families, who live at or below poverty levels who do not feel privileged. In fact, they feel angry and disenfranchised by the very system they feel should be taking care of them. They were mostly invisible before Trump gave them a voice, as disingenuous as his action was, because he is the epitome of white privilege. The cultural face of poverty, prison, inner cities, and low-paid jobs is a black face, even though it is not an accurate depiction of overall poverty in our country. That face becomes the only face of an entire race in America, effectively erasing the real diversity found in black Americans. This disconnect causes many white people who are in situations of poverty or low-paying jobs to change their personal narratives and to believe that while they are in their circumstances for valid reasons, blacks are not.

They vote conservatively because of racial bias, hurting themselves while being punitive to people who they believe are not deserving of help, a kind of cyclic self-punishment.

Other white people believe they are not racist, but they don't want to have any kind of conversation where they have to spend most of the time listening instead of stating what they believe. They refuse to see there is another experience out there that does not fit in their narrative of self-defined success and heightened status. Such narratives make them uncomfortable and feeling vulnerable to losing what they feel they have single-handedly achieved without the assistance of white privilege.

Ronald and I are repeatedly asked, "Why does everything always happen to you?" or "What did you do to cause that?" Or, we've been told that our experiences are not true, can't be true, that they could never happen.

The answer to all those offensive accusations, because that is what they truly are, is that millions of other people of color have similar or worse experiences. Many paid the ultimate price of inequality through the loss of their lives or lost loved ones. In many ways, we have been fortunate compared to other interracial couples and people of color, but that doesn't diminish or erase the incredible opposition we've experienced in our lifetime together, and that Ronald has endured as an individual.

Until we can have an honest conversation and make substantial systemic changes to our infrastructure, nothing will change. Taking down the stars and bars and some monuments won't make the changes we need to have happen, especially now, when a Trump presidency is openly racist and xenophobic.

Small changes will make people feel good, and, unfortunately, lead many to believe their work is done.

When SCOTUS ruled in favor of the subsidies for the Affordable Care Act, the Fair Housing Act, and same-sex marriage in June 2015, I felt encouraged. Those decisions continued the journey to a level playing field for all people in our country. But now, once again, such advancements are being systematically erased by a Trump presidency.

We have a lot of work to do. I won't strike back in anger, but I will continue to work for change and progress. Stand united, resist, persist, and shout "No more" to keep going in the right direction. Small successes, like the removal of those flags and monuments, do not undo centuries of racism and inequality, but they help keep us moving forward.

Chapter 17
#AltonSterling #PhilandoCastile

In July 2016 I was immersed in the election campaign, still believing Trump would never be elected, and debating and sharing mostly with my liberal friends—by then, most of my conservative friends no longer spoke to me, or I to them. I never thought I would be that person. I always enjoyed having a diverse group of friends, friends who could never gather all together in one room at the same time, because they would have spent the whole time judging and shouting at one another.

I am an optimist. If I weren't, I might not have made it through my childhood with an alcoholic mother. I might not have made it through the years when the world thought our interracial marriage was wrong and acted to prove it. I might not have picked up and moved from a familiar place to a new place with a new culture—from North to South. From a place where immigrants are common, to a place that takes pride in its generations-long heritage, no matter how violent, oppressive, exclusionary, and divided it was.

My optimism keeps me going.

But on July 4, 2016, I lost my optimism. Independence Day. The day I became certain America was not the America I felt promised when President Obama was elected.

I mourned over so many senseless, violent, terrorist acts, and the lives lost to them in Brussels, Orlando, Istanbul, Dhaka, and Baghdad. I held my breath, anticipating the next tragedy.

At home a vile, negative presidential campaign was building up to the conventions taking place later that month. It was a cult of personality: a clash between reality and reality TV; between the truth of progress and the lies of racism, hatred, misogyny, fear, and illusion; and between two different visions of America's past, present, and future.

Daily, I felt assaulted by the Trump campaign's messages and the comments of his supporters. There was no political correctness on their parts, just plain discriminatory and hateful messages. Yet they came from the self-righteousness of disenfranchised, mostly white people who were impacted by a rigged system—a system rigged in favor of the white and wealthy and against everyone else, although there is a hierarchy of the disenfranchised, with white males on top and women, people of color, and LGBTQ people at the bottom. Unfortunately, Trump supporters were laying their hope on the very person who epitomized the unfair system of privilege.

Then I heard about a shooting in Baton Rouge on July 5, 2016. A citizen notified police that a man in a red shirt was selling CDs in front of a convenience store and had threatened someone with a gun. Police arrived on the scene and tased Alton Sterling. Then, two police officers pinned him to the ground. One of the officers pulled his gun and shot Alton in the chest six times, execution style. Alton Sterling was 37 years old. He was the father of five. After they shot and killed him, they pulled a gun from his pants pocket. I watched the mother of his oldest son speak to the media at a press conference called by the local NAACP, religious leaders, and elected city officials. I watched his fifteen-year-old son cry unabashedly in front of the cameras—a child full of despair, who lost his father and has the video of his execution burned into his brain. A child who is no safer on the street than his father was.

Just one day later, on July 6th, Officer Jeronimo Yanez, of the Saint Anthony, Minnesota, police department, stopped Philando Castile, 34, for a broken taillight and asked him to produce his license and registration. Even though, under Minnesota law, Castile had no duty to inform the officer unless asked, that he was licensed to carry and had a gun in the car, he still let Yanez know. Things quickly soured after that, as Yanez repeatedly yelled at him not to reach for the gun, and both Castile and Diamond Reynolds, his fiancée, assured Yanez he was not reaching for it. Then Yanez pulled his gun and fired seven times at close range, killing Castile. Reynolds began live-streaming soon after the last shot was fired. Her four-year-old daughter sat in the backseat behind her. As the world watched and the police officer became completely unhinged and unfit for duty, I concentrated on Diamond Reynolds, her voice steady, intent on documenting Castile's murder. She said, "Stay with me, we got pulled over for a busted tail light in the back. And the police just he's, he's, he's covered. He, they just killed my boyfriend."

Philando's murder reminded me of one of our many police stops. We were driving across the state of Florida in February 2001. We had visited family in Sanford, and then were heading west to Bradenton and Tampa to visit more family and for Cara and Mackenzie to audition for placement in a high school dance conservatory. There were wildfires and we had to drive hours out of our way in order to avoid the interstate, which had closed due to poor visibility. In rural south central Florida, the roads were narrow, and fruit pickers and cattle seemed dangerously close to the cars. We discovered there were few gas stations along this route and at one point, we were close to running out of gas completely when we finally came upon a small, aged gas station, circa 1960. Then we were lost in a small town, circling around the town square, and trying to figure out which road the GPS kept announcing for our turn: "Recalculating." Ronald saw lights in the rearview mirror.

"Here we go," he said, as he pulled to the side of the

road.

Cara and Mackenzie were in the backseat. They were sixteen. We sat waiting for the officer to approach the car. When he did, all I could see was his utility belt, his large gut, and his gun.

"Is this your car?"

"Yes," Ronald answered, his hands tightening on the wheel where he had rested them at 10:00 and 2:00 so they were clearly visible. He was driving our sundance gold Acura CL, which we had dubbed "the pumpkin car" due to its rare color—only 900 of them were manufactured.

"Are you all together?"

"Yes."

"I'm his wife and these are our daughters," I added, hoping the clarification would make him leave us alone.

"License and registration."

Ronald announced where they were stored and that he was going to retrieve them. Cara, Mackenzie, and I sat rigid in our seats. I recently asked Cara if she recalled the incident. She did, and she said she was confused by the officer's questions. "Of course, we were all together. We are a family," she said as she related her memory of it.

I watched Ronald grow agitated as the cop took his time back in his patrol car, looking him up, seeing if he was a criminal. Wondering if he could charge him, or maybe tell him he wanted to search the car. Wanting to let the drawn-out minutes increase our anxiety. Ronald's fingers began to squeeze and release. His right hand went to his nose, rubbed across it, went back to the wheel, then back up to his nose. I knew the sign. His anger was roiling just under the surface, looking for a fissure, ready to break loose as soon as it was found.

He regularly worked with cops in his job as a firefighter. He knew the good cops and he knew the bad cops, the ones who looked for trouble and who thought they knew a bad guy by skin color alone. He could stand up to them when he was in uniform. Tell them what they could and couldn't do at a scene under his command. But in his own car, without his uniform to clearly show his equal status, he was vulnerable. We all were. His vulnerability angered him.

"Don't let him get to you," I said, my voice shaking. "He isn't worth it."

I wondered why he didn't produce his badge. It would have immediately de-escalated the situation. He told me later it was an unfair advantage over other people who endured such stops, and that is why he wouldn't use it. He disavows privilege of any kind, whether it is due to status or skin color. The cop would have to deal with only the information at hand and his own bias.

Ronald's hand returned to the wheel. He took a deep breath, settled back in the seat, kept his hands on the wheel.

The officer returned to the window. "Where are you going?"

"West. We were lost and having trouble navigating through this square. I wasn't sure what turn to take."

"Did you know you were in a school zone?"

"No, I did not."

"Next time I'll ticket you. I don't want to see you again."

"You won't."

He will not call cops "sir." He wouldn't do it on the fire department either. He called his superiors by rank, captain or chief. Calling white men "sir" is too reminiscent of Jim Crow and white men calling black men "boys" while expecting black men to address them as "sir," a sign of their self-imposed superiority. Castile's fiancée, Diamond Reynolds, used the term, telling the officer, "Yes, I will, sir. I will keep my hands where they are. Please don't tell me this.

Lord, please, Jesus, don't tell me that he's gone. Please don't tell me that he's gone. Please officer, don't tell me that you just did this to him. You shot four bullets into him, sir. He was just getting his license and registration, sir."

It was well past school hours when that officer stopped us in Florida, and even if it weren't, school was in winter recess. That was his excuse for stopping us. He really wanted to know why a black man had three women, one obviously white, and two racially ambiguous teenagers, in an expensive vehicle. Was he a pimp? Had he stolen the car? Each of us let out a long breath. Ronald started the car and we drove off, never looking back. "Don't sweat the one that didn't get you," Ronald pronounced. Two decades later, I am reminded the outcome could have been very different, and I am chilled by the images my mind draws, taken from the graphic police video and Diamond Reynolds' live-stream video. We traded the car in about a year after that stop because Ronald was repeatedly pulled over when he drove it. Its unique and, at the time, rare color, attracted constant police attention, and we worried his luck was running out.

As Reynolds' stoicism begins to crumble on the live-stream video, her daughter is heard saying, "It's OK. I'm right here with you." That sweet child's voice still haunts me and reminds me that even the littlest people of color are forced to shoulder the largest of burdens, burdens that would terrorize and ruin most of us. Burdens I know my daughters carry, too.

Police video released in 2017 show another officer yanking the child out of her seat through the window, the girl wailing in fear. Protect and serve? Not if you are black.

My old optimism was crushed beneath the weight of ongoing Jim Crow.

How is it that some people can support President Trump and support a military-style, vigilante-style police presence in predominately ethnic minority communities?

Racism is alive and well. Jim Crow is thriving. Individuals unaffected by racism pretend it doesn't exist. Yet their subconscious racial bias supports systemic racism. Often, they blame the targeted group, people of color, as being unfit and unworthy of equal treatment.

The Sterling case was turned over to the FBI and the Federal Department of Justice, but the burden of proof is so strict in these violent and murderous police stops that very few are prosecuted. When Jeff Sessions was confirmed as attorney general, I saw no clear path to justice. The Baton Rouge police chief, Carl Dabadie, refused to fire Officer Blane Salamoni, who killed Alton Sterling, and he remained on paid administrative leave as of the end of May 2017.

Officer Jeronimo Yanez, who killed Philando Castile, was charged with second-degree manslaughter and two felony counts of dangerous discharge of a firearm. Yanez was acquitted of all charges on June 16, 2017. His lawyer, Earl Gray, said the state never had a case and that his client "wants to get on with his life." What does it take to prove excessive force? Castile's mother was disappointed, saying, "The system in this country continues to fail black people and will continue to fail us."

The song *Strange Fruit*, sung evocatively in 1939 by Billie Holiday, documented lynching in the Jim Crow South. It was originally a protest poem, written by Abel Meeropol. More than 4,000 African-Americans were lynched between 1877 and 1950. Lynching was a terror tactic to keep blacks subjugated, segregated, and marginalized.

> *Southern trees bear a strange fruit*
> *Blood on the leaves and blood at the root*
> *Black bodies swingin' in the Southern breeze*
> *Strange fruit hangin' from the poplar trees*
>
> *Pastoral scene of the gallant South*

Another Day in Post-Racial America

The bulgin' eyes and the twisted mouth
Scent of magnolias sweet and fresh
Then the sudden smell of burnin' flesh

Here is a fruit for the crows to pluck
For the rain to gather, for the wind to suck
For the sun to rot, for the tree to drop
Here is a strange and bitter crop

Now bodies are left lying on concrete, often uncovered, surrounded by police tape, growing stiff, families and communities barricaded away: all plainly meant to warn people of color what will happen to them, too, if they forget their marginalized status in society.

I still want to feel that small kernel of hope in my heart. It may seem unbelievable. Yet I want to believe humanity will acknowledge inequality, discrimination, and supremacy and want to stop it all, because it is the right thing to do.

I felt this longing after crying my way through *Free State of Jones*, which we saw on Independence Day, the day I stopped being optimistic. The truth is, human beings are complex, feelings are complex, and we often have conflicting feelings about the world around us.

The film is about Newt Knight, a white Southerner who deserted the Confederate Army because he believed it was a rich man's war, fought by poor men. He also assisted the Union Army, embraced slaves as his equals, and raised an American flag at the courthouse of the Jones county seat in Mississippi, one of the most historically racist states.

After watching Alton Sterling and Philando Castile die over and over on the news, I started researching Newt Knight and found an article on him from *Smithsonian Magazine*. It parses out the true story from the poetic license of the movie and what writer and director Gary Ross went through to make the film.

Joseph Hosey, a forester in Jones County, and an extra on the film *Free State of Jones*, said, when interviewed for the article, "When you grow up in the South, you hear all the time about your 'heritage,' like it's the greatest thing there is. When I hear that word, I think of grits and sweet tea, but mostly I think about slavery and racism, and it pains me. Newt Knight gives me something in my heritage, as a white Southerner, that I can feel proud about. We didn't all go along with it."

Many other community members of Jones county considered Newt Knight "what we call trailer trash."

John Cox, a member of the Sons of Confederate Veterans, said, "I wouldn't have him in my house. And like all poor, white, ignorant trash, he was in it for himself. Some people are far too enamored of the idea that he was Martin Luther King, and these are the same people who believe the War Between the States was about slavery, when nothing could be further from the truth."

I find it interesting when wealthy white people claim that it is poor people who are crafty, unreliable with the truth, and in it for their own self-interest, when they are often the ones who change the truth to benefit themselves as often as possible, as when Cox said the Civil War was not about slavery. President Trump exhibited that same distinction of changing the truth every time he stepped up to the podium during the 2016 presidential campaign and spun his version of America.

Reading the article on Newt Knight lit the coals of my optimism. It wasn't because the history of Jones county and Newt Knight was clear and simple. His story reveals our country's complex history and who we are as a people, inclusive of all Americans, not just some.

Newt Knight, his life story, and the story of his mixed-race descendants, reminded me that there are people who can move beyond systemic racism, the craziness of segregation, and self-righteous superiority.

There are people who, like me, refuse to turn a blind eye or accept an unfair system based on skin color, and who refuse to be silent. They understand that the country and its relationship with race are complex, but they don't give up. They are quietly heroic, and sometimes loudly and violently opposed to the directions our country took and continues to take. They tell the stories of race in our country even when Hollywood can't believe anyone would be interested, and there may be no money in producing such films.

Together, we can challenge those who refuse to see the truth of our country and who will not acknowledge the systemic racism that supports white supremacy and privilege and makes life dangerous and deadly for people like Alton Sterling and Philando Castile. We can challenge President Trump and the ignorance he is peddling like a carnie peddling snake oil.

Newt Knight continued to be a true rebel, even after death. He asked to be buried next to Rachel his black, common-law wife (He never divorced his first wife, and interracial marriage was illegal.). She had been his grandfather's slave and, with her, he fathered five children. It was illegal for whites and blacks to be buried side by side in Mississippi, but he ended up buried next to the woman he loved for eternity.

My optimism dove again during the first 100 days of the Trump administration. Trump's election to president, his campaign platform, which included racial ideology, white supremacy, and racially charged language, his appointment of individuals with proven records as white nationalists and supremacists, and his inability to deliver comforting words after racially motivated hate crimes, have caused anxiety, fear, extreme disappointment, and hopelessness in reaching an America that embraces and practices equality. And it keeps getting worse, from children being separated from their parents at the border to lies about how building a wall will protect the country from criminals and rapists.

I realized Trump's America in which I live. It is motored by hatred and fear, and the system is tipped in the favor of some, while the path for others is broken or rubbed out.

I want to believe we Americans are better than police, vigilantes, and terrorists who are slaughtering people of color. How many of you feel fear every time your spouse or child leaves the house, because you are afraid he won't come home? That he might be stopped by the police or by some neighbor who thinks he doesn't belong, and possibly killed? Every single time Ronald goes out the door, I think this way, even when I go with him, because I know I cannot protect him.

This knowledge doesn't make me want to give up. It makes me want to try harder.

Newt Knight's gravestone tells the story: "He lived for others." May each of us one day be able to claim that truth.

Chapter 18
America Broke My Spirit

I turned the news off for two days in September 2016 because I realized I had it on almost 24/7. I had found myself constantly anxious and viewing strangers with suspicion. I talked about my anxiety on Facebook to the discomfort of my FB friends. Both my daughters had reported crying and anxiety, too. Ronald was agitated. I needed a break. We all did.

When I turned the news back on, I discovered bombs went off in New York and New Jersey and a black man was shot and killed in a police stop after his car broke down in Tulsa, Oklahoma.

One of the pilots in the helicopter circling the scene at the Tulsa police stop said "... Looks like a bad dude. Might be on something." But I didn't see that. In the video taken from the helicopter, Terence Crutcher was walking slowly with his hands in the air. He did not appear dangerous. Nor did he have anything in his hands. Later police claimed he might have had PCP in his car, the usual criminalization and thugification of the victim. His twin sister, Tiffany Crutcher, said, "He didn't have a chance to live."

Crutcher, 40, did not deserve to die that day.

Then one day later, on September 20, 2016 in Charlotte, North Carolina, Mecklenburg police officer Brentley Vinson shot and killed Keith Lamont Scott, allegedly for carrying a gun. His family disputed this, and many witnesses came forward to say he read in his car each day, though no book was found in the car on that day. It was later confirmed he had a gun strapped to his ankle on the day of the shooting, but there was never proof that he drew the gun, or even reached for it. He also had a traumatic brain injury (TBI) from a motorcycle accident, and he had just taken his medication. Police videos were not immediately released. Protests broke out, and when police arrived in riot gear, violence erupted. One person was shot and killed, not by a police officer, and his name and the circumstances of the shooting were not released at the time.

North Carolina had passed a law that went into effect on October 1, 2016. The law makes it nearly impossible for the public to obtain access to police video. I believed the authorities were dragging their feet waiting for the effective date so they would not have to release the video.

North Carolina is an open-carry state. People can wear a weapon to the grocery store, to restaurants, walking down the street, and sitting in their cars. Exceptions include government buildings and any businesses that post signs that guns are not allowed. How can anyone be shot for carrying a gun, when it is perfectly legal? Easily. Just like the stand-your-ground law in Florida is for white people like George Zimmerman, open-carry is for white people in North Carolina and in other open-carry states. In 2017 one more gun bill, HB 746, circulated in the North Carolina state legislature. This bill, if passed, would make it legal to conceal a weapon for anyone 18 or older in places where carry is allowed, which is almost everywhere. Currently, to carry concealed, an individual must be 21 and acquire a conceal permit, eight hours of safety training, and pass a test of skills at a shooting range. Eighteen-year-olds cannot legally drink alcohol, but they may be able to carry a concealed weapon if the state legislature can push the bill through. Again, this is not a law for black Americans; it is a law to arm white Americans. This is how Michael Hill, president of the League of the South, put it, in February 2017:

> [T]he League of the South is calling for all able-bodied, traditionalist Southern men to join our organization's Southern Defense Force for the purpose of

helping our State and local magistrates across Dixie combat this growing leftist menace to our historic Christian civilization. As private citizens in a private organization, we will stand ready to protect our own families and friends, our property, and our liberty from leftist chaos. Moreover, we will be ready to assist our local and State authorities in keeping the peace should they find it necessary to "deputize" private citizens for that purpose.

America is for white people, at least in the eyes of the far right, white supremacists, and the Trump administration.

Some positive news filtered through my veil of tears and anxiety that fall, but my lightened mood would be short-lived. Officer Betty Shelby, the officer who shot and killed Terence Crutcher, was charged with first-degree manslaughter. Though this gave me solace at the time, she would later be acquitted and then hired at another police department. On September 23, 2016, Rakeyia Scott, Keith Lamont Scott's wife of twenty years, released video taken on her cell phone of the shooting. I felt this release would pressure the authorities to release their cam footage, and they did on October 4, 2016. None of the videos showed a clear narrative, but Rakeyia Scott's video continues to haunt me.

After viewing it repeatedly, crying as I listened to her words meant to diffuse the situation and calm the police, who should have been responsible for de-escalating the situation, my sorrow reached a terrible place. I wondered how strong must a person be to record, hold herself still, put aside the terror raging inside her, engage calmly with the police, and watch them murder her husband in cold blood? Why must she be that strong? Because in America, it is a must. The whole legacy of black American history is to not let them, the white men, break you. I don't know if I could be that strong. But I know I have to think about it because I may have to be one day, unless we can stop the senseless murder of black men and women. Sadder to me still was that officer Vinson is a black man. Did he truly feel threatened, or did he buy into the stereotypes often recalled when dealing with black men? No charges were filed against him.

Protests in Charlotte, despite a call for a state of emergency and a midnight curfew, remained absolutely peaceful on the third evening, though the marching went well past midnight. These protests continue to be an important voice in the fight for equal treatment and justice. North Carolina Congressman Robert Pittenger said of the protesters, "The grievance in their mind is the animus, the anger. They hate white people because white people are successful, and they're not." I am so tired of people like President Trump and others who call black Americans poor, uneducated, resentful, angry, lazy, needy, and criminal; any negative adjective will do. My family, my interracial family, is full of educated professionals. They own homes and cars and buy their own food and go on vacations. My black friends, (and I don't just have one for kicks), are educated professionals, too, though I have certainly known poor people in my life. I was one of them, growing up in a white suburb outside Albany, New York.

As a child, I felt on the fringe of mainstream white America, far afield from the clapboard houses with white picket fences shown on TV, with mothers in starched aprons, high heels, and pearl necklaces, and fathers coming home after work in suits and ties, briefcases in hand. This is the America to which the conservative white Christians are trying to return, when middle class whites enjoyed unprecedented economic prosperity on the backs of the poor, the uneducated, and minorities.

In my house, a boomerang hung over the kitchen threshold and a black plaster aborigine sat on the knickknack shelf in the parlor. The Infant of Prague statue, dressed in red and cream finery, stood at the center of my dresser top, a stuffed koala bear, made from real koala fur, next to it.

Ma wore housedresses and vinyl slippers, and Dad came home with shirts soiled with newspaper print from handling bundles of papers in the mailroom where he worked. His face always had a five o'clock shadow, the whiskers making him look swarthy. He carried the afternoon newspaper, which he would read in its entirety that evening, folded under his arm. He washed up and shaved a second time each day before coming to the supper table.

Dad spent his weekends tinkering with the engine of the car he bought used and that he hoped to keep running for as many years as possible. Ma read novels, watched old movies, smoked cigarettes, drank hot tea all day and cold beer all evening, and yelled at the kids in the neighborhood. "I'll cut your bloody head off if you do that again," she said when one boy threw dirt at the mutt we kept chained in the backyard. The police arrived soon after, because the boy's mother thought Ma meant it. Maybe her Aussie dialect seemed threatening.

I looked different than the little children at the feet of the blond-haired, blue-eyed Christ in the picture on the wall of my Catholic Sunday school classroom. I had skin as white as snow, but my dark hair and amber eyes made me look foreign in comparison.

My parents were older than the parents of my schoolmates. Most people could not pronounce my last name.

We ate pasta and Italian bread to satisfy Dad, or boiled dinners like ham and cabbage to please Ma's palate. I liked both with equal zeal. When I heard the neighbor tell my mother she grew up calling Italian bread "WOP bread," I felt the same shame I felt when I heard other kids call Brazil nuts "nigger toes." Even if I did not know what the words meant, I could hear how unclean they were in the way they were spoken, spit out with disgust. When my parents fought, usually on a daily basis, Ma often said Italians were barbarians, trying to hurt and diminish Dad. I don't know if she understood how badly it made me feel.

What I understand now is that we closely resembled white, working-class Trump supporters, though my parents tended to embrace liberal views. Back then, however, there were jobs for that class of workers that paid just enough to purchase a small, post-World War II home, built especially for war veterans and their growing families, along with a used car for work and toting the family around. Some years the house paint was chipped and the grass brown, because Dad could not afford paint and grass seed. The unpaved driveway, the only one on the street not paved, was uneven and the stones covering it were dangerous for little knees and elbows when I rode my hand-me-down bike over the ruts. But the house was ours, the last mortgage payment made just one month after Dad passed away at age 69. Poverty looks a lot different today.

White people don't know how offensive it is when someone assumes you are poor, uneducated, and criminal just because your skin is brown. And it doesn't matter where you live, what car you drive, or what your profession is. If you have brown skin, America views you differently. This goes for many white liberals, too, who believe in magnanimous equality, in theory, but revert to stereotypes in practice, and who also, consciously or not, support systemic racism.

Racial bias is rampant in America. It is hard to deny. I turn again to the story about my homeowners' association and the white supremacist attorney Crews who performed legal services for the organization. My own neighbors chose a white supremacist over Ronald and me, and we lived there for ten years. I was president of the HOA. I did good things for the neighborhood, and Ronald kept our yard and garden in tiptop shape. Yet, when I discovered the attorney was the

North Carolina chapter chairman of the League of the South, the other officers decided to retain him as an attorney and accept my resignation from the board of directors. Their loyalty lay with someone we paid to represent the HOA in legal matters, just like we paid someone to mow the common areas, rather than with me, a neighbor. Most people did not even know the attorney's name. Some may not have even realized we needed an attorney. But the HOA officer, who refused to replace him, and who accused me of "just wanting a black attorney," said the white attorney was more than just a person who was paid to perform legal services, he was "part of the HOA; one of us," and not a single neighbor disputed that statement.

Not us, though. Despite our living there for ten years, I think they made it clear that we weren't part of the neighborhood. We were interlopers. We are liberals who don't understand Southern culture, white Southern culture, where white men are superior, and everyone else is submissive. We lived someplace they didn't think we belonged. Black families don't belong anywhere in America, because white people don't want them.

Another neighbor, who lived behind us, got angry when Ronald indicated they had directed their drainpipe on to our property, causing flooding. She blurted out—unrelated to water issues—"You think everything bad happens to you because you are black. You are a dumbass."

Ronald said, "Interesting that you are the one who brought that up, and not me."

Secretary Clinton was lambasted for calling half of Trump supporters a "basket of deplorables." She was not far off, as she has a brilliant mind for numbers and statistics.

From an NPR story:

... A PPRI/Atlantic poll this spring found that Trump supporters are more likely than others to say that:

1. The U.S. is becoming too soft and feminine (68 percent);

2. It bothers them when they encounter immigrants who do not speak English (64 percent);

3. The government has paid too much attention to the problems of blacks and other minorities (55 percent);

4. Men and women should stick to more traditional gender roles and tasks (50 percent);

5. Discrimination against women is no longer a problem (46 percent).

If anything, Secretary Clinton may have been purposely underestimating the number.

The worst thing, what I keep replaying in my head, is when a few neighbors told me I was wrong calling attorney Crews a racist. They deemed he was not racist. Would they change their minds if they knew he participated in the Unite the Right rally in Charlottesville, and where he ended up being a part of the group that beat Deandre Harris unconscious? My thoughts on the topic were not credible before the rally. I am certain they were not credible when Crews appeared in a front-page story of our local paper, regarding his charge that Deandre attacked him.

Here is a portion of another blog post from Michael Hill, who is the national founder and president of the League of the South, the organization the attorney chaired in North Carolina:

> But [multiculturalism] is really not about ushering in equality among all races, religions, and cultures; rather, it is about destroying Western Christian civilization, the world's premier unmitigated evil. And because the South is the strongest enclave of this civilization, it finds itself square in the crosshairs of the MC crowd. Why do you think the Feds are not willing to lift a hand to stop our dispossession by a floodtide of illegal immigrants? It is the continuation of

Reconstruction to the ultimate degree. We are being replaced as a people. Any attempt by Western man to defend himself and his civilization is called "racism," and is designed to paralyze him completely (even when no malice is shown toward any other group). This agenda points up the fact that the proponents of MC seek not fairness, justice, or equality but demonization and destruction of the white, Christian West. Only whites, and white Southerners in particular, are not allowed to have a country all their own. Asia for Asians, Africa for Africans, but no South for white Southerners!

All indications point to the success of the MC agenda of paralyzing the West through guilt manipulation. Though we never had any sort of debate about whether we wanted to be a MC polity, it has been forced upon us anyway. Anyone who protests is silenced by the usual epithets. Even opposition to illegal immigration is enough to get you called a "racist" or a "xenophobe." If you don't believe me, check out the Southern Poverty Law Center's rants on the subject.

The xenophobic, racist, extreme right wants to get rid of political correctness, but it can't stand to be called what they are, and that is white supremacists. My neighbors were quick to tell me I didn't know what I was talking about. They were quick to blame my ignorance on "that liberal organization," the Southern Poverty Law Center. But, oh, don't go calling them a basket of deplorables.

White supremacists flocked to support Trump. They haven't felt so emboldened since David Duke, once the grand wizard of the KKK, ran as a presidential candidate in 1988— does anyone else even remember this? Duke decided to run for a Senate seat in 2016 because of Trump's popularity among white supremacists.

Here is a snippet of an interview with Steve Innskeep of NPR:

[David Duke] was confident that Trump backers in

Louisiana would support his Senate run. (He was wrong. He lost.)

"We've already polled inside the Trump voters, and we know that we're going to carry 75 to 80 percent of those who are going to vote for Trump," he said.

Steve asked, "You think Trump voters are your voters?"

"Well, of course, they are!" Duke said. "Because I represent the ideas of preserving this country and the heritage of this country, and I think Trump represents that as well."

On that point, Duke was right. At the August 12, 2017 Charlottesville, Virginia, neo-Nazi and white supremacist protest, he said, "We are determined to take our country back. We are going to fulfill the promises of Donald Trump. That's what we believed in, that's why we voted for Donald Trump. Because he said he's going to take our country back. That's what we gotta do."

President Trump's unscheduled rant about the Charlottesville violence, delivered on August 14, 2017, where he accused both sides of being to blame, proved he is just fine with white supremacist support.

Black men get shot and killed if they are found in white neighborhoods, even when they live there, and they get shot and killed in predominately black neighborhoods, the police acting under law-and-order rule instead of protect-and-serve. No place is home if you are black in America. No place is safe.

White people can't imagine it. They get angry. Why do you keep talking about race? They blamed President Obama for being divisive.

Trump campaign chair Kathy Miller said, "If you're black and you haven't been successful in the last fifty years, it's your own fault. You've had every opportunity; it was given to you," and she also called Black Lives Matter "a stupid waste of time."

Then she blamed Obama, saying, "I don't think there was any racism until Obama got elected. We never had problems like this ... Now, with the people with the guns, and shooting up neighborhoods, and not being responsible citizens, that's a big change, and I think that's the philosophy that Obama has perpetuated on America."

She resigned shortly after, playing the scapegoat in a campaign rife with hatred and ignorance.

She is one of the deplorables, and there are many more where she came from, including the white supremacist protesters.

You know what hurts and outrages the most? When family and friends choose white over acknowledging that what we experience is different than what they do or when their own discomfort takes precedence over ours.

I remember going out to dinner with my Aunt Josephine, my father's sister, a few years before she passed away. She had been against our relationship, like my parents, and had stopped speaking to me for years, until our daughters were born. She had read a story in one of the tabloids about biracial twins where one was born black and the other white. She called my sister and asked her what we would do if that happened. My sister assured her we would love them. But her curiosity remained strong, and when the girls were about five months old, she came to see for herself. It was enough to reestablish our relationship. Unfortunately, that would not be the case with my parents, who also did not speak to me and who both passed away before we were able to fully resolve our estrangement, and before Ronald and I were married in the Public Safety building in front of the judge after traffic court on a Saturday morning, and before we had our daughters. After my aunt visited to check on the girls, we stayed in touch regularly, and even more so when she was elderly. I never forgot how she was a steady and stable presence in my chaotic childhood, and I wanted to show my love and appreciation. Both Ronald and I gently addressed her various faux pas over the years, like when she referred to Ronald as "you people."

On this night, my aunt, Ronald, our daughters and I had gone out to eat dinner at a restaurant in the town in which I grew up. When we stepped into the lobby, my aunt bumped into two old friends, who were on their way out. There was an awkward silence as they gawked at us. My resemblance to my aunt was probably obvious, as was Cara and Mackenzie's resemblance to me. Ronald's presence must have been downright shocking, both women looking from my aunt to him and back again as no words were forthcoming. One woman, her hand to her throat, finally asked, "What is this?" Aunt Josephine, stumbling over her words and visibly reddening, as if she had been caught in a deed so vile she would never repair her reputation, did not introduce us, mumbled a hastened "good to see you," and quickly ushered us over to the hostess' station. I turned to look back and saw her friends staring at us in disbelief and seemingly unable to move. Her friends caught her participating in something they found outrageous and egregious, and her embarrassment was due to their witness, and not because they were rude to us.

One male relative recently unfriended my daughters and me on Facebook after one daughter posted a microaggression she experienced, and he had counseled her not to read race into every situation. A diverse group of female professionals responded, as did I, telling him he was offensive for questioning her understanding of the situation, and the relative ended the discussion and our friendship by saying, "I will not apologize for being a white man." My other daughter hadn't even participated in the discussion, but he unfriended her, too. I don't need anyone to weigh in on how they perceive the situation. If you haven't lived it, you have no idea.

I am sure some of my Facebook friends wonder why I still talk about the HOA incident on occasion. Why am I still emotional, and why haven't I put to rest the whole issue because the attorney and the other officers resigned, and then we moved? Why is it a fresh wound that won't heal?

Because I know how those neighbors felt about us.

As soon as the police pull over a black man in a traffic stop, he is already considered not one of them, "looking like a bad dude" just for having brown skin. That's what racial bias does to one's perception of an individual. Even when the police officer is black, as in the Charlotte shooting, racial bias plays a part. How can having a broken down car, a broken taillight, or maybe "fitting the description," which was the original reason for approaching Keith Lamont Scott, turn so deadly, so quickly, and in so many stops?

Don't tell me not to mourn. Don't tell me my tears and anxiety are only hurting me. Don't tell me things aren't dire. Don't tell me it only looks bad because the media are drawing attention to it.

Maybe my anger scares you. Your unwillingness to be outraged scares me.

I am not asking you to give away your sense of status and privilege as a white American. I am only suggesting it should be available to every American.

You know what would be nice, though? Maybe saying what my friend on Facebook said to me back in September 2016, when I was feeling low. She said, "You're not alone. I can't fight your fight, but I can struggle along in my own way." Thank you.

Chapter 19
I Am Tired of Talking about Race and Gender, Too

Whenever life got difficult for me as a child, and that was fairly often growing up with an alcoholic mother, I gave myself a pep talk. I do it in adulthood, too, when life seems overwhelming, or seems to go against my grain. I remind myself that everything is temporary, and if it is temporary, I can get to the other side of it and come out fine. It is usually a big enough push to motivate me through the worst life throws at me.

But on November 8, 2016, I started sinking fast. I fell down the rabbit hole, hard. Each announcement on election night pushed me farther down. I could not believe what I was seeing. I swore at the TV and slapped the chair. Ronald was mostly silent. Then he said, "It's over."

"No," I said. "They haven't called Florida yet. Surely she will take Pennsylvania." But soon I, too, realized it was over, despondency and dread taking root in the pit of my stomach.

Although Secretary Clinton won the popular vote by more than 2.8 million, she lost the Electoral College vote. Although we had heard of Russian interference in October, the full impact of the revelation had not yet sunk in. The last time a candidate won the popular vote but lost the election was in 2000. Al Gore won the popular vote by 500,000. Admittedly, some odd things occurred during the Bush/Gore election, including those mysterious hanging chads in Florida.

Over the next couple of weeks, attempting to digest the news that Trump would be the next president, I commiserated with other progressives, argued with those who take a conventional and closed-minded approach to life, shed a lot of tears, and expressed anger when talking to my immediate family.

I could point fingers: it was the fault of the third-party voters and/or the fault of the 50 percent of the voting age populace who chose not to vote. Certainly, Russia interference played a role. All in all, Trump won on less than 25 percent of all possible votes. But now that I find us here, how is blaming others any good? It won't change the outcome.

As I watched the parade of appointments, including Steve Bannon, Mike Flynn, and Jeff Sessions, men who have demonstrated racial hatred and other extreme conservative views, I felt like I was being suffocated in the rabbit hole. Then there were all the racially motivated attacks, graffiti, tweets, bullying, and other acts of white supremacy that continue under a Trump administration. Trump's lack of responses and his inability to recite unifying words of comfort on the one or two occasions he has responded, turned the rabbit hole into a black hole.

I couldn't even see the rabbit hole exit from that far down.

I've talked and written about racism for some forty years, but more so in the last ten years. We plunged into the hole when President Obama was elected and the far right decided, when they could not find any real scandals to bring President Obama down, to systematically attack his validity, credibility, and character. The birther conspiracy, supported and carried on by Trump, caused all kinds of racist responses. Claims he was Muslim did the same. How did we arrive at a place where, against Constitutional protections, candidates for presidency must be avowed Christians?

But Americans got tired of being accused of being racist and they responded... with more racism. Nothing better than accusing the victims of being responsible for the hatred and oppression heaped on them. Then America voted in Trump, the candidate openly endorsed by the KKK. And almost all the Trump supporters expressed anger at being called racists. However, they did not disavow the hate crimes that popped up around the country after the election, over 1,000 reported, though not all verified. A good number of the people perpetrating these crimes were avowed Trump supporters.

People are saying they are tired of hearing about racism. Quite a few contend racism didn't exist until President Obama started talking about it. People who believe that have short memories and a poor understanding of our history.

Every time we made racial strides in our history, there has been an equal or stronger backlash. President Obama's election in 2008, and his list of accomplishments, caused the rise of the Tea Party and the rise of Trump. Hatred is strong, even when it is only inside the hearts of a minority. Silence by others makes it even stronger. Silence is complicity.

In the past, black towns, successful places with black-American-owned businesses and commerce, and segregated from white towns, were burned to the ground and black Americans were lynched. Greenwood, Oklahoma, known as Black Wall Street, was one such town among many. Linda Christenson wrote this about the white mobs that descended upon Greenwood:

> The term "race riot" does not adequately describe the events of May 31–June 1, 1921 in Greenwood... In fact, the term itself implies that both blacks and whites might be equally to blame for the lawlessness and violence. The historical record documents a sustained and murderous assault on black lives and property. This assault was met by a brave but unsuccessful armed defense of their community by some black World War I veterans and others.
>
> During the night and day of the riot, deputized whites killed more than 300 African Americans. They looted

and burned to the ground 40 square blocks of 1,265 African American homes, including hospitals, schools, and churches, and destroyed 150 businesses. White deputies and members of the National Guard arrested and detained 6,000 black Tulsans who were released only upon being vouched for by a white employer or other white citizen. Nine thousand African Americans were left homeless and lived in tents well into the winter of 1921."

After Japan attacked Pearl Harbor on December 7, 1941, Japanese-Americans were rounded up and placed in internment camps. They lost their freedom and everything else, including their homes, businesses, careers, and, in some cases, their lives, because white Americans believed their loyalty would lie with Japan, even when they had been Americans for generations in some cases. America offered restitution to the survivors of internment in 1988 under the Civil Liberties Act.

Black American descendants of slavery and Jim Crow have yet to receive restitution.

Today I argue that the discrimination and hate crimes of contemporary America are as bad as ever. Lynching may have been the method of terrorizing and controlling black Americans in the past, but police stops that end in murder are just as effective. A lot of white Americans disagree. In a national survey conducted in 2016 by Emily Ekins of the Cato Institute, 68 percent of white Americans hold favorable views of their local police departments, while only 40 percent of black Americans hold favorable views.

I can tell other white Americans that I am tired of talking about racism, too, and misogyny, homophobia, xenophobia, and religious intolerance. But I must talk about them because they are not going away, and at this time in our history, with the election of a racist, misogynist, and religiously intolerant president, it is getting worse. I am also tired of people supporting systemic racism and the other "-isms," but pretending denial, as they did when they voted for Trump.

We are losing our freedoms, including freedom of the press, freedom to protest, and the freedom to be fully participating American citizens. This should scare the shit out of people, but many instead celebrate how the people they hate are finally paying, confident somehow that they themselves are excluded from this loss of freedoms. Many more are silently compliant.

Some of my extended family members are worried that my speaking out will result in imprisonment. I jokingly told my mother-in-law to visit me in prison and bring cookies, (I have been bringing her home-baked cookies when we visit her up North), after I am arrested for political activism that includes this book, my blog, my Facebook posts, and writing to my congressmen.

But maybe prison for political activists is not such a distant reality, and maybe we are close to another McCarthy era, when people's lives were ruined or lost because the government didn't like their politics. Doug Ericksen, a Republican state senator in Washington, was considering a bill that makes certain kinds of protests a felony. (Right now, one can be arrested for blocking traffic or causing property damage, but both are misdemeanors.) He called certain protests "economic terrorism" because they disrupt businesses. Such a law would not only result in a possible prison sentence or probation, it could revoke the individual's right to vote. Think about that and the number of protesters who came out for Black Lives Matter, against a Trump presidency, and against white supremacy after Charlottesville. Even though no such law was passed, and if it were, the Supreme Court would surely rule it unconstitutional, it was terrible to even consider curtailing peaceful protests.

A professor at Rutgers University, Kevin Allred, who is white, was picked up by police at his Brooklyn home for tweeting, "Will the 2nd amendment be as cool when I buy a gun and start shooting at random white people or no...?" Of course, the answer to his rhetorical question is "yes," as demonstrated by the response to the December 14, 2012, Sandy Hook shooting, where twenty six-year-olds were massacred, and with each mass shooting after that one. Even though calls were strong for sensible gun control legislation, none ever made it to the legislative floor.

The police delivered Allred to a psychiatric hospital. Although extreme racial bias is still not considered a mental illness, apparently, political activism is. My extended family members may not be overreacting.

So there I was, quite a few e-mail exchanges with Senator Thom Tillis on record, other e-mails penned to Senator Richard Burr, Representative Virginia Foxx, and Speaker Paul Ryan; a growing number of outraged and angry Facebook posts logged; and my writing, which usually helps me sort through my thoughts and feelings. Yet I was still reeling.

What if Trump's cabinet were filled with racists, misogynists, homophobes, the religiously intolerant, and xenophobes? Will Trump's rant to "make America great again" or, as many of us say, "white again," become reality? The answer to the first question is, "It is," and the answer to the second question is, "Yes, if we don't resist and persist."

Will we be living in a country where political activists are jailed, people of color and women are second-class citizens, separate and unequal, Dreamers will be deported to a country in which they don't remember, children will be snatched from their parents' arms and left in detention centers for months on end while others will never be reunited with their parents, LGBTQ individuals will be subjected to conversion therapy, women will have to ask their male partners permission to take birth control, or perhaps will go to jail if they get an abortion, Muslims will have to register as such with the government for possible deportation or internment, all of us will be forced to worship under fundamentalist dogma, and citizens will be encouraged to demonstrate their hatred toward any group that is not compliant or white and heterosexual?

My panic just soared past the moon. Time for a pep talk, and I gave it on Facebook on November 19, 2016. Here it is:

This country needed HRC. The majority of voters realized that, even those who didn't think she was perfect. We lost, more than just the election, as we are seeing in these days of transition of power. But we cannot give up, not for one moment, because of all the people who came before us and refused to lie down and take oppression and violence and segregation and economic hardship and second-class citizenship. In their honor and for the future generations, we have to keep going forward while the white nationalists, white supremacists, misogynists, homophobes, reality TV stars, and powerbrokers try to force a vision of America on us that we know is shameful, hurtful, ignorant, and finished the moment we stand against it. Stronger together.

I realized something else in the days after the election. I was in mourning. Watching the Medals of Freedom ceremony made me see it. The last eight years under an Obama administration weren't easy because of the strong opposition, but they were a promise. President Obama was a promise of a different America, led by a man who embodies grace, perseverance, intelligence, humor, and a view of what a truly egalitarian America would look like, an America in which my family is just another American family. I would have still missed President Obama terribly if Secretary Clinton had won the election, but I would have looked forward to her chance to lead us toward a truly progressive America, taking up the gauntlet we handed to President Obama in 2008. Instead, we elected a horrid, self-centered, self-aggrandized, entitled reality star, who doesn't respect women, minorities, people with disabilities, the free press, and anyone else who doesn't adore him. He doesn't respect the rule of law. He is a monster who uses threats and tweets to bully and who is fully taking advantage of hatred to promote nothing but his brand and his businesses. If he had a shred of ethical and compassionate thought, he would stand before America in a press conference devoted to just this topic, and tell America that white supremacy and white nationalism are abhorrent treason. He would fire the white nationalists, like Stephen Miller, from his White House administration. Instead he averred that there was violence on all sides, minimizing the damage and destruction that hate and fear can cause. He has repeatedly been silent after reports of racial hate crimes. I am in mourning for more than the term of Obama's presidency. I am in mourning for the loss of our country to haters and supremacists who are no better than Dylann Roof and the white supremacist organizations like the League of the South and the KKK. When you must debase others to feel better, you are lacking in character and quality, and you have no right to drag the rest of us down with you.

Yes, I will get through this, and you will, too, but it will take hard work, the ability to speak up loudly and often, and perseverance in the face of unprecedented obstruction. There is a way to climb out of this rabbit hole, and that is to keep talking about race and gender, no matter how tiring it gets, until we no longer have to do so. Just consider this time in our history temporary, and soon we will be on the other side of it. We got this.

Chapter 20
Countdown to 2020

We are at a precipitous time in our lives and in the history of our country. As the president exhibits bizarre behavior and the Mueller investigation team hands down more and more indictments, a sense of dread hangs over the heads of many progressives. Maybe many of you feel as I do: depressed, angry, anxious, and fearful, with a sense that the world tilted on its axis and something is coming to an end. The weird reality is both sides of the partisan aisle feel that way. The right feels it looking back over the Obama years, and the left feels it while living through the Trump years as we witness an end to progress.

Instead of letting these uncertain times fill us with anxiety, it is important to act and to remember what progress looks like, including a vision of America where everyone is equal and each individual's life matters.

At the end of 2016, I listed some possible New Year's resolutions, so we could try our damnedest to right the runaway train before the inevitable crash.

But calling them resolutions is not quite comprehensive enough for determining the future of this country. Resolutions seem like good intentions that don't have to be fulfilled. Plus, they cannot possibly fix all that is broken in our country. They cannot possibly lift me, or us, out of the rabbit hole. They cannot possibly stop the inevitable train wreck a Trump presidency is bent on causing.

Rather, I decided to call them living commitments. They are for individuals and for the collective America we all call home, although not every single one will apply to every person.

1. Appreciate the people in your life who love you just as you are. Love them back just as unconditionally. Don't just

tell them you love them. Show them every day through kindness, compassion, attentiveness, and concern. And when life gets in the way and the situation feels dire, help, if you can, if they accept your help, or sit and listen. Let them vent, and vent, and vent, until they feel better. One day, you will need the same.

2. Stay fit and work toward maintaining good health, but don't get obsessed about it. Sometimes, it is just as important to treat yourself and to have a good time. Everything in moderation isn't such a bad adage.

3. Stop believing your time and your life are worth more than others'. Especially stop believing your skin color or your religion makes you better. The world isn't as big as it used to seem, and we are all in it together. We are all exactly the same at birth, imperfect and trying to survive. We are equal in every way. The differences are our life circumstances and the cultural and ethnic beliefs in which we are raised and through which we view the world around us. So even the people you may think do not deserve equality are your equals. Treat others as you would have them treat you.

4. Speak up as often as necessary and do not let this Trump circus become normalized with excuses or pleas to "give him a chance." He's blown all his chances, and then some. He is an egomaniacal, ignorant, bigoted, ethically challenged, sexually inappropriate, greedy, developmentally stunted, rich guy who will destroy our country, and possibly the world. Remember what Maya Angelou said: "When people show you who they are, believe them the first time." Don't be complacent.

5. Read the real news from the free press: *The New York Times*, *The Washington Post*, or any of the major metropolitan newspapers and your local paper, so you know what is going on in your area. Learn which outlets are fake news outlets, and don't support them by reading or sharing

their trash. Stop watching news entertainment channels like Fox News. They make money by making you view the world through fear, paranoia, and hatred.

6. Get involved with your local politics. Be an informed voter, pass out flyers, help people register to vote, make phone calls, or think about running for office—we need people to run for office. Look how successful we were in November 2018. We elected the most diverse pool of candidates in the history of our country. At the very least, get out and vote in every single election and write to your representatives at all levels so they know what their constituents are thinking. We need to get out there and get the word out that hate and insularity are not our mandates. Equality and quality of life for every single American are our mandates.

7. Remember technology has shrunk the size of our world and it is important that we engage in the global negotiations among countries, global human rights, and the global economy. We are a world power, though we may not be for long. President Trump has it wrong, very wrong, and his ignorance and reliance on white supremacists, crazy, old, white generals who believe in conspiracy theories, and possibly Russian president Vladimir Putin, could very well stir up world unrest. He has already stirred world unrest with his amateur and bullying ways among world leaders and his impulsive and uninformed decisions, like pulling out of the Paris climate agreement, trashing NATO members, and playing playground bullies with Kim Jong Un. World War III is now a possibility, and it won't be like the other wars, which were horrible, devastating, and inhumane in their own rights. President Trump already demonstrates an inability to keep national secrets confidential. A war under the Trump administration could end it all, especially since Trump tweeted about a nuclear arms race, and because there are

other unstable, egotistical, world leaders like him. Do you really think they believe all people matter? You are delusional if you think they do.

8. Speak up against discrimination of any kind. The worst you can do is nothing. It makes you complicit. Even if you don't think it is your problem, it is, because it is our country's problem. There are people who are oppressed socially, educationally, and economically because of the color of their skin, gender, sexual orientation, religious beliefs, or abilities. Studies show prejudice and oppression are bad for people's health. Inequality is making some Americans ill and shortens their lives. A *New York Times* article stated, "Research suggests that discrimination is internalized over a lifetime, and linked to a variety of poor health markers and outcomes: more inflammation and worse sleep; smaller babies and higher infant death rates; a greater risk of cancer, depression and substance use. The cumulative burden of discrimination is linked to higher rates of hypertension and more severe narrowing of important arteries in the heart and neck. Even the telomeres at the end of our chromosomes, which act as a sort of timer for aging cells, can shorten."

Do you think it is okay when one group feels perfectly comfortable defining the worth of other people based on a single standard, (white, male, heterosexual), and then treats others differently, indifferently, or even violently? If you don't, then don't be silent.

9. The only reasonable response to the murder of unarmed black men and women is outrage. Think of it as the new Jim Crow control of the black population through terrorization, akin to lynching prior to the Civil Rights movement. If you don't feel outrage every single time you see such murders on the news, ask yourself why you think their lives don't matter. If the answer is racial bias, which it probably is, work hard and learn how to overcome it and to

acknowledge that not everyone experiences America the same way you do. It is important that we recognize, acknowledge, and question our biases. If we don't, our country will never overcome systemic racism, sexism, homophobia, ageism, classism, and discrimination against people with disabilities. We will never reach the ideal of equality. America is becoming more brown and female and white males are no longer the majority, nor should they be the only people who are in positions of power. Will we become majority minorities with a white male ruling class, or will we get this figured out so that every American is bestowed freedom equally, has a voice in the process of governing, is protected under the law, and where we can truly govern our country for the greater good, and not for the good of the few?

Don't just feel the outrage. Do something about it. Write to your representatives, the current Attorney General— Jeff Sessions already changed the mandate of the Department of Justice before he resigned—and the police departments that switched from protect-and-serve peace officers to militarized population control. And if you are thinking we should care as much about the police who occasionally get gunned down, I agree. But let's get real: some people are going to snap when they fear walking down the street or having a broken taillight could result in death by police officer. Can you imagine living under that kind of stress? It feels unbearable, right? Until we retrain police to be peace officers, who are invested in community policing and demonstrate the ability to de-escalate situations, and police departments reflect the ethnic makeup of communities they serve, that kind of over-the-top retaliation may still occur. So, this is about the safety of all parties involved. Yes, all lives matter, but we are focusing on black lives because those are the lives that appear to have no value in our society.

10. Stop pretending our economy and the middle

class are reliant on manufacturing jobs. Technology has changed manufacturing, and those jobs, as well as coal mining jobs, are gone, not necessarily shipped out. Our economy is renewable energy, technology, consumer, and service-based. Pay a living wage and allot full-time status to those jobs that were traditionally reserved for high school students. Let unions negotiate pay, benefits, and workers' rights and safety again. We need unions and the strength of their membership numbers to make working conditions better for everyone. A rising tide lifts all boats, no matter their sizes.

11. Fight against privatization of government functions. The government doesn't have to make a profit. Running the government like a business is a terrible mistake. Private companies do and want to make money, lots of it, through methods that put the bottom line above all else, like quality, affordability, and accessibility of service. Medicare, Social Security, Medicaid, the US Post Office, and the Internal Revenue Service are government functions that are almost wholly self-sustaining. The maintenance of prisons should also be a government function—a privatized prison system is only profitable when the prison is full beyond capacity, which means ridiculous sentences for petty crime. Health care should also be a government function—a single-payer system that can negotiate drug and health service pricing, focus on preventative health care, include dental care, and take the burden of providing health insurance to employees from corporations that complain the cost is too much. If the system were government run and single-payer, corporations could spend more on jobs. Don't let rich (mostly) white men, hoping to get richer, take over such functions. They are more interested in making money than in serving the interests of the public, and services may not be equitably distributed or accessible to all people. Furthermore, the middle class is filled with government workers. Privatize

those jobs, and the middle class will shrink even more.

12. Public education should remain public education. Vouchers are just a way to ensure wealthy people can send their children to private schools using public school funds instead of their own money. Their advantage will disadvantage our children. It will never be equitable, and the same goes for the privatization of public schools.

13. Stop feeling like you worked harder than other people to get where you are. Realize most Americans work hard, and being punitive about pay and benefits is a horrible way to treat fellow Americans. Assigning more worth to one job over another is wrong—we need all kinds of jobs to make our country function, and all jobs deserve at least a living wage. Many people benefitted from systemic and institutional racism and sexism to get where they are, so they are not better or harder workers, but privileged. Most people want to work, and there should be jobs for them that pay a living wage. Place a cap on executive pay, so that a CEO's pay is not more than fifty times the lowest-paid employee of the company. (Right now, it is 300–400 times higher). For those who can't work, provide living wage assistance.

14. Stop being punitive to poor people. Most of them are poor due to systemic classism or racism. Poor white people, (many of whom live in rural areas), outnumber poor black people because blacks make up only 12 percent of the total population, and less than 28 percent of them live in poverty. Racial bias makes most people believe blacks make up the majority of poor people. We can help all poor people by making sure they have access to education, jobs, health care, housing, and food. Not a single child in America should go hungry or without a warm bed or a safe place to live and attend school. Our tax dollars should support safety nets and access to the inherent rights listed above. Relying on churches and charities is wrong, because they do not have enough to

help all the needy and sometimes, they are subjective about whom they serve. Think of your tax dollars as tithing. Such a small amount of tax dollars covers safety nets. (The majority of tax dollars are spent on defense.) So, taxpayers should not feel they are helping freeloaders, who are a definite minority among the poor.

15. Remember that patriotism is not just blind allegiance to our country, the president, or the flag. It is the active participation and contributions one makes as a citizen that is true patriotism. Participation can include respectful and peaceful protest, such as taking a knee during the anthem. If you are in support of the Confederate flag, you are not a patriot, and you are guilty of treason. White supremacy is a myth and your support of it, or your support of a supremacist president and his supremacist cronies, goes against the best ideals of this country and is a damaging testimony regarding your character.

16. Equality doesn't take away from some to give to others. It simply ensures equal access and opportunity to reach one's God-given potential. No one will take your jobs, your guns, (except maybe assault weapons which have no business being used by anyone not in the military), or your religion from you. That is the lie you've been told so you will vote for the wealthy to get even richer. In fact, equality will ensure you have the freedom to live, work, socialize, and worship as you choose, and it ensures it for every person. Realize that if a person decides to marry someone of the same sex, for example, that decision in no way impacts your religious rights. If you decide your religion prevents you from assisting in the formation of such a union, then please don't run for the position of city clerk or have a business which daily puts you in conflict with your religious beliefs. That is something you must personally decide upon, while not imposing your will on others.

17. Remember this country has enough room and resources for everyone here, including illegal immigrants and their children, many of whom were brought here by large corporations, like Trump's businesses, so they could pay them lower wages and not provide benefits. Our diversity is our strength. That's what true democracy is: the cacophony of many ideas and perspectives in order to find the best path to serve the greater good.

We will get through this time in our history just as we struggled, fought for, and won progressive change in the past. We will head toward the righteous and progressive path and be on the right side of history, even as other forces try to turn us backward. Let's turn our anxiety and despair into action. America is already great, and together we can make a difference and make it even greater.

Chapter 21
Not the Last Chapter

I had already decided to write this book before Donald Trump was elected as president. The Mothers of the Movement motivated me to make my own small contribution to the national conversation about race. Their narratives, strength, and sacrifices moved me.

But if I were worried about the state of our country before Trump's election, I'm near hysteria now. The conservatives relish being in power again, despite the daily scandals, incompetence, ignorance, arrogance, conflicts of interest, indictments, and possible obstruction of justice of this administration. They have dropped all suggestions of standards in favor of power, or else they could never have accepted as their standard bearer a blustery, unqualified, developmentally stunted, compulsive liar and reality star shouting about making America great again, which is code for "make America white again." Hillary Clinton was right when she opined that half his supporters are deplorably racist and xenophobic.

When former Attorney General Jefferson Beauregard Sessions came out with a statement about penalizing sanctuary cities through the loss of Justice Department grant money, my fears were validated. Sessions was also the bearer of the news that President Trump decided to rescind DACA, leaving 800,000 children of undocumented immigrants concerned about their status, and that of their parents, in the only country they remember. Another action taken by Attorney General Sessions, equally insidious, was to delay the federal consent decree negotiated among the Loretta Lynch-led Justice Department, the Baltimore police department, and the city of Baltimore, Maryland. Sessions' mandate was not equal and fair treatment under the justice system, but law and order—codification of the new Jim Crow—and making sure black and brown lives continue to matter less. I am worried his successor will not be better.

The Baltimore consent decree, and those negotiated with other cities and police departments, was put in place to hold the police accountable through the reduction of police misconduct, including profiling and use of excessive force. The decree was negotiated because of overwhelming evidence of excessive force and racial bias. Baltimore city officials, recognizing a problem, invited the Department of Justice to investigate. Attorney General Sessions believed such oversight of police departments is best left to the states and to the police departments themselves, even though many states and police departments have proven otherwise.

The case that prompted the Baltimore investigation and consent decree was the arrest of Freddie Gray, 25, on April 12, 2015, for what his family claimed was "running while black." The police, after they tackled him, found a knife in his pocket. This is not illegal in Baltimore. Still, they shackled him and packed him into the back of a police van on his stomach. He was not secured by a seat belt. Evidence emerged that the driver took him on what was called a "rough ride" that likely tossed the trussed young man around the back of the van as the driver rushed through pot holes and other bumpy patches. Freddie called out for help. He did not get it. Police found him unresponsive in the back of their van at the end of the ride. He died from a broken neck where his spinal cord was nearly severed. Days of protests and riots, as well as media exposure of the problems plaguing black, inner-city Baltimore followed. These problems included unequal economic and social resource distribution between affluent and poor neighborhoods, and they put Freddie's murder into the national spotlight. Six officers were charged with an assortment of crimes, but none were convicted. Five officers faced internal disciplinary hearings in late 2017. The Justice Department declined to levy federal charges due to lack of evidence.

The list of men, women, and children assaulted or killed by racially biased police, vigilantes, and white supremacist terrorists keeps growing, and it includes 66-year-old Timothy Caughman, a retired social service worker, stabbed with a sword in Times Square on March 20, 2017, by James Jackson, 28, a white military veteran from Baltimore who wanted to "practice killing a black man." The killer told authorities he planned on killing as many black men as possible because he was tired of seeing so many white women dating them. He thought the white women would think, 'Well, if that guy feels so strongly about it, maybe I shouldn't do it."

I found his thoughts on misogynistic control of white women, through the murder of black men, chilling. In my forty-plus-year-old interracial relationship, I've met men like him, men who told me I could do better, men who frightened me with their intense interest even after it was not returned, and men who thought I was damaged and, therefore, an easy conquest. They thought I should choose them, and, in doing so, save my reputation.

Timothy Caughman was able to walk to the closest police station before collapsing and dying.

James Jackson pleaded guilty on January 23, 2019. His conviction is the first in New York to fall under the "murder as a crime of terrorism" statute, and he will serve life in prison without parole.

New York Mayor Bill DeBlasio said this about the hate crime: "More than an unspeakable human tragedy, this is an assault on what makes this the greatest city in the world: our inclusiveness and our diversity. Now it's our collective responsibility to speak clearly and forcefully in the face of intolerance and violence—here or across the country. We are a safe city because we are inclusive. We are a nation of unrivaled strength because we are diverse. No act of violence can undermine who we are."

Trump didn't have a word to say about this terrorist killing in the city he calls home, though he speaks out against Muslim terrorists regularly. Leonard Greene of the *New York Daily News* said:

> *"But in the time since a racist rode a bus for three and a half hours from Baltimore to Trump's hometown to hunt down a random black man with a sword the approximate length of my arm, not a single word has rolled off President Petty's fingertips.*
>
> *Not a 'terrible.' Not even a 'sad.'"*

In 1989, when a white woman was brutally raped in Central Park, Trump spent $85,000 on full-page ads in four of New York City's major newspapers, calling for reinstatement of the death penalty against the four black boys and one Latino boy who were charged with the crime. Known as the Central Park Five, they were cleared by DNA evidence in 2002, and awarded a $41 million settlement for wrongful convictions. Trump was not deterred. The truth seldom deters him. After the airing of a 2012 documentary on the five, he tweeted, "The Central Park Five documentary was a one-sided piece of garbage that didn't explain the horrific crimes of these young men while in park." He deemed the settlement "the heist of the century."

Sarah Burns wrote in a *New York Times* op-ed on October 17, 2016:

> *"Mr. Trump has also suggested that the teenagers were guilty of something that night because... 'these young men do not exactly have the pasts of angels.'*

None of the Central Park Five had ever been arrested before, so Mr. Trump's reference to their pasts has no basis in truth. The five were in the park that night, but they maintain that they did not participate in other attacks, and there is no evidence that they did.

So we are left with Mr. Trump's presumption that because they were black and brown teenagers from Harlem, they must have committed a crime.

... Mr. Trump owes many people overdue apologies. At the top of his growing list should be Mr. McCray, Mr. Wise, Mr. Salaam, Mr. Santana and Mr. Richardson. They were victims of a rush to judgment 27 years ago. They shouldn't still be."

Trump owes an apology to someone else, too, and that is former President Barack Obama. In 2011, he jumped into the birther fray, announcing on *Good Morning America*, "I have some real doubts. I have people that actually have been studying it, and they cannot believe what they're finding... Maybe [his birth certificate] says he's a Muslim."

In 2012 he tweeted, "An 'extremely credible source' has called my office and told me that [Barack Obama's] birth certificate is a fraud." He encouraged candidate Mitt Romney to bring up the matter during a debate with President Obama, tweeting, "In debate, [Mitt Romney] should ask Obama why autobiography states 'born in Kenya, raised in Indonesia.'" Trump's use of alternative facts began long before Kellyanne Conway coined the term on *Meet the Press* on January 22, 2017.

Trump kept the conspiracy alive in 2013, tweeting, "How amazing, the State Health Director who verified copies of President Obama's 'birth certificate' died in plane crash today. All others lived."

As a candidate, he tried to dodge questions about President Obama's birth certificate: "Who cares right now?"

In 2016, without a hint of apology, then-candidate Trump declared President Obama a citizen, as if Obama needed his stamp of approval as proof of his legitimacy.

President Trump has always shown us exactly who he is, and how he regards the rest of us, particularly people of color, women, and the poor. His list of which lives matter is short. When a man wielding the power of the president's office is silent about racially and xenophobic-inspired hate crimes and hate groups or who claims both sides are to blame, the damage to our country may become irreparable.

On May 20, 2017, Richard Collins III, 23, a commissioned second lieutenant in the Army who was set to graduate college a few days later, was stabbed to death while standing at a bus stop in College Park, Maryland, where he was visiting friends. Killer Sean Christopher Urbanski was a member of a Facebook group called Alt-Reich, a site filled with white supremacist content, but as of publication, he had not been charged with a hate crime.

Black men have become victims of systemic racism and racially motivated oppression and violence in other ways. The North Carolina Center on Actual Innocence (NCCAI) has worked to release black men serving life sentences for crimes they did not commit. Men like Darryl Hunt, who was charged with raping and murdering a white woman in Winston-Salem. He spent nineteen years locked up, before he was proven innocent and released.

While trying to piece his shattered life together by assisting with other cases of wrongful conviction, he was found dead on March 13, 2016, in his friend's borrowed car from a self-inflicted gunshot wound. He had prostate cancer and depression.

Others include Kalvin Michael Smith of Winston-Salem, who was prosecuted for assault with a deadly weapon with intent to kill and armed robbery in a brutal 1997 attack on a pregnant white woman who now lives with twenty-four-hour assistance because of severe brain injury. Smith spent almost twenty years in prison for a crime he says he did not commit. After years of appeals and advocacy to overturn the conviction, he was released in December 2016 because of a reduction in his sentence due to an omission of evidence during his trial. His conviction was not overturned, even though no physical evidence ever linked him to the crime scene, and two witnesses later recanted their testimony. Freedom has been difficult. In March 2017, he was shot in the back in what he thought might have been an attempted robbery. He almost died. Worse is that he is recognized wherever he goes, and people have not been kind. Some think he was awarded a large financial settlement for wrongful conviction, but that isn't true. He was only released, with nothing but the clothes on his back. In late August 2017 police issued a warrant for his arrest for misdemeanor assault of a female after an argument broke out between him, his girlfriend and her friend, who tried to stop it. Smith turned himself in the next morning.

Half-brothers Henry McCollum and Leon Brown, from New Jersey, were visiting their mother in Red Springs, North Carolina, in 1983, when they were charged at ages 19 and 15 of raping an 11-year-old-girl. Both intellectually disabled, they spent thirty years in jail awaiting justice. Their restitution upon release was $750,000 each. That works out to about $12.00 an hour had they worked those years.

There are thousands of other wrongful convictions across the country, many in states with legacies of Jim Crow laws, and often, the men leave prison with inadequate restitution, as if any amount of money could replace lost years and mitigate their suffering and that of their families. They were released, yes, but with no prospects and little assistance in making a transition to civilian life. Many others die in prison waiting for justice. We failed them.

The Trump administration, from his first day in office, has been governance by distraction, threats, tweets, lies, obstruction, and executive orders, ruled behind the scenes by white supremacists like Steve Bannon and Stephen Miller. But even after Bannon was fired at White House chief of staff John Kelly's urging, Trump is the same man he has always been. It is no wonder President Trump has no words to comfort the families of black men killed by racially biased police officers, vigilantes, and domestic terrorists. His chaotic approaches and incompetence are stunning, especially coming off former President Obama's term. The differences are remarkable, including how each has responded to crises in America and the world and how each approached the hard task of comforting and uniting us.

I've thought for hours about how we arrived at this place in history and how we must pick ourselves up and continue the march toward equality and progress. What we are experiencing now is the very real backlash of electing a black man to the highest office in the country. President Obama's election was not the path to post-racialism we envisioned. History shows a pattern of advance and backlash again and again, every time we have made strides toward racial equality.

I've cried, lost sleep, and worried about how many more men, women, and children of color I will hear about in the news, victims of a racist system and society, victims like 15-year-old Jordan Edwards. He was shot and killed in Balch Springs, Texas, on April 29, 2017, my twin daughters' thirty-third birthday, while the car in which he was a passenger was leaving a large house party. The officer who shot him claimed the car was backing toward him, but body cameras proved the car was leaving the area. The police officer was fired and charged with murder.

I've feared the Black Lives Matter movement and its objective to bring police brutality to light would be swept to the side because so many competing priorities—Russian interference, nuclear warfare, unregulated pollution, deconstruction of the federal government, collusion with a foreign power, obstruction of justice—came to the fore during this chaotic presidency.

Yet President Trump found time to attack the NFL players who took a knee during the anthem in support of Colin Kaepernick and the Black Lives Matter movement. Kaepernick was the first player to take a knee in quiet protest of systemic racism and in support of Black Lives Matter. President Trump abused the power of his position when he called the players "sons of bitches" and suggested the team owners fire any player who exercised his right of free speech. He claimed the protests were unpatriotic and disrespectful to the military, another dog whistle to the extreme right and his white supremacist supporters. This was not surprising, as he has repeatedly been soft on white supremacist protesters, calling some of them "very fine people," and critical of those protesting against systemic racism, police brutality, women's rights, health care, and his administration. It backfired, as many team owners linked arms with their players to show their support, but Kaepernick remained unsigned in the 2017 and 2018 seasons, and the divisive controversy continues as some teams require players who won't stand for the anthem to remain in the locker room.

Liberals have been labeled snowflakes in this crash course that points to despotism by an egomaniacal white supremacist and misogynist. Trump's cabinet is the whitest and most male-dominated since the Reagan administration. The number of positions in the Trump administration filled by individuals with no experience and knowledge, who harbor extreme right political agendas, who are mired in conflicts of interest, unethical behaviors and criminal activity, who are billionaires and have forgotten or never known what it is like to be poor or middle class, and who are opponents of the very mission of the departments to which they have been appointed, is frightening.

Black Americans know about being silenced. They know about the demonization and criminalization of their communities, and the racist, and historically violent, responses to demands for equal treatment. But many white liberals are not used to circumstances that seem completely out of our control. The privilege of having a voice and our credibility not being called into question has been intact, until now. We are not snowflakes, and we are certainly not enemies of the country as the far right often tries to paint us, but we do suffer mental and emotional trauma from the inexplicable unraveling of our democracy. Black Americans have lived with this kind of trauma generationally, since their ancestors were packed onto slave ships.

This time in our history parallels the social revolution of the 1960s, when liberal white college students learned the power of protesting by watching and then collaborating with black organizations fighting for social justice, equality, voting access, jobs, and integration. We need that now, too, through the support of and collaboration with Black Lives Matter and other organizations, like Moral Mondays in North Carolina. It is disingenuous to expect the victims of oppression to fix the problem by themselves, because it means the oppressors don't have to do or change anything. Instead, as a country, we need to ask: how can we help, what needs to change, and how can we change? Then we need to listen and act.

What kind of country do we envision under a Trump administration when war and wealth for the few are the endgames, foreign adversaries are subverting our democracy and putting our national security at risk, and executive orders are slashing the rights, safety, care, and support of our citizens, future citizens, and visitors?

It is the kind of country that doesn't care when black men, women, and children are slain, contained, and oppressed by a militarized police force with a mandate of law and order. It is the kind of country that regulates which lives matter and which ones don't. It is the kind of country where white supremacists believe they can come armed to a rally, chant "Blood and soil" and "Jews will not replace us," and where they celebrate the murder of Heather Heyer, a white woman, because, as one KKK grand wizard proclaimed after the Charlottesville protest, "I'm sorta glad that them people got hit, and I'm glad that girl died. They were a bunch of Communists out there protesting against somebody's freedom of speech, so it doesn't bother me that they got hurt at all." It is the kind of country that widens the wedge between classes, and where the path between them, the one taken by those from lower classes to higher classes, is blocked or destroyed. It is the kind of country that legally stops women from controlling their bodies and making reproductive health decisions. It is the kind of country that turns its back on refugees fleeing untenable lives of death, chaos, poverty, and oppression. It is the kind of country that snatches children out of the arms of their parents and locks them in cages and then cannot figure out how to reunite them. It is the kind of country that exploits the white rural vote but doesn't serve those voters, forgetting them after their votes are counted.

The last nine years have made me think about subcultures and tribalism in our country. They are the reason we often can't find the compassion and empathy we need for other groups. We see no common ground and feel no connection, understanding of, or loyalty to them, and they become dispensable, even deplorable, while we fight for what we think our tribal needs are. We seem unable to value people from other tribes. Eric Trump, a guest of Sean Hannity on June 2, 2017, said of liberals and opponents to his father, "I've never seen hatred like this. To me, they're not even people." Dehumanization is a tactic oppressors have used throughout history, including slave owners and dictators like Hitler, who referred to Jews as rats. Besides, where was Eric Trump during the last eight years, when Tea Partiers and his father attacked Obama's legitimacy?

Ronald and I saw the movie *Hidden Figures*, the story of the black women behind the computations that put our rockets and astronauts in space and brought them safely back to earth. They endured segregation and disrespect in the workplace. I want to know about these wonderful stories of perseverance and achievement, but they depress me. In talking to Ronald about the film, I found the words to express my sadness. If NASA had celebrated these women, given them credit for their contributions, and told America about how extraordinary they were, we might be less likely to be living in a place today where women still make less pay than men for the same work and blacks are sometimes eliminated from the hiring pool just based on their names, even when their qualifications are the same or better than other candidates. Black individuals in positions requiring higher education, intelligence, judgment, and leadership might have been normalized if this story, and the many like it, were told. These women were unique in their skills and application of their intelligence, but not unique in that they were intelligent and able, and that's a truth America needed to hear.

Instead of spreading the lie of inferiority of the black race to maintain a system of privilege for white citizens, the stereotypes could have been dismantled and disproven in real time, not sixty years later. We have not done the right thing because of tribalism.

Ronald was one of the first black firefighters hired on the Syracuse Fire Department in 1981 after a federal consent decree in 1978 ordered the department to align hiring practices with the demographics of the city. He became the third black lieutenant in the history of the department, but it did not come easily, and not because he did not have leadership skills or was not a competent firefighter. It was because his predominately white firefighter brothers could not imagine relying on a black officer to lead them into danger and to make competent, split-second decisions needed to save lives at a fire scene.

When Ronald interviewed for the promotion to fire lieutenant, the chief, under the guise of joking, said, "Did you study or did you just get lucky?" referring to the exam he took to qualify.

It incensed me because I knew how seriously he took his career, how important his service to the community was to him, and how hard he studied for the exam. When he first got on the fire department he tried to study in the library at the station, but the officers in charge often found reasons to keep him away from the study materials or the materials mysteriously disappeared. The white guys on his shift studied together as a group, but closed the books if Ronald entered the room. So he bought his own materials at a hefty cost and studied on his off hours. He deserved that promotion, even after one of the other black firefighters let him know that he overheard a district chief saying he would do everything he could to cause him to fail his probation. He underwent additional scrutiny and was measured against unfair standards compared to what most white probationary officers experienced. But it didn't stop him. He passed probation. When he finally retired, after twenty-five years on the job, at my urging, because I felt his luck was running out, and I also saw how the job changed him, he said, "I never got to enjoy being a firefighter. They made sure I didn't."

Today the chief of the Syracuse Fire Department is a black man, who stands on the shoulders of the black firefighters who went before him and who demanded equal opportunity in an institution that was structured to exclude them.

I believe we can be members of more than one tribe, and recognize American subcultures based on ethnicity, region, and urban/suburban/rural experiential lifestyles. We can all be members of a tribe called Americans. Sure, there are lots of subtribes, but we don't have to hurt one population of Americans to uplift another. That's an old lie we have been told and spread that separates us and helps politicians. As the adage goes, a rising tide lifts all boats. Respectful recognition of subcultures will help us remember our humanity and make every person feel valued. It will dampen bias and promote empathy and understanding.

Many people don't realize we are all ethnic. In some ways, the push for DNA testing by genealogy sites helps promote this idea. White and black are just social constructs, but what country and culture are your ancestors from? How and when did they migrate? Was there a history of forced migration? What traditions, foods, and rites of passage were passed down to you? In my family, my Irish-Australian mother was as likely to make a boiled dinner of ham and cabbage as she was to make manicotti or lasagna to please my Italian father. I never tasted kielbasa, tacos, fried rice, sauerbraten, fried chicken, coleslaw, or liverwurst as a child, yet some of my classmates who did begged for an invitation to a dinner of spaghetti and meatballs at our house. The closest they'd ever gotten to the real thing was a can of Chef-Boyardee. Black, Latino, Asian, and Native Americans are equally diverse and depend on what country of origin, or tribe, their ancestors came from for their traditions. Americans can easily learn about those subcultures and experience them through access to different ethnic foods, festivals celebrating diversity, and the media. These can open minds.

Acknowledging our diversity and understanding that mainstream culture is shaped by it, makes it okay to be different, because we all are. There is no big block of white people and smaller blocks of black, Asian, Hispanic, and Native American people. But we've allowed that construction of sameness within groups, segregation from other groups, and the subjective designation of what groups are good and bad, to create a system of privilege and to validate our biases.

Regions and whether you live in an urban, suburban, or rural area also matter in individual perspective. If you live in the city and you lose your job, difficult as that is, you can usually find another job, even when transportation is an issue. (My daughter who lives in New York City often complains the trains are late or not running, and the news media report that the system is antiquated and unable to adequately handle the 5.9 million passengers who ride it each day.) If you live in a rural area and the major industry, like coal mining, closes down, there aren't any other jobs to be had, and many people don't want to leave land that has been in their family for generations. Maybe you live in the suburbs and have three or four choices of grocery stores close by, while inner-city folk may only have access to the corner grocery shoved into the first floor of a 200-year-old building and have limited choices and high prices. Rural residents may have long drives to the closest Wal-Mart.

We all have worries, and when they press in on us, we may see them as more important than those of others. Or we look at others and underestimate the severity of their problems, like overcrowding and high rents in urban areas and lack of resources in rural areas. If we rely less on personal biases, ("I'm afraid of big cities," or, "I'd be bored out in the middle of nowhere,") and more on listening to how it really is for people who live differently than we do, we can be more open to those differences, and perhaps more willing to see how much we are alike. More importantly, we would learn empathy for other people whose worries and hardships are brought about by differing circumstances.

When we remember that most of our ancestors came from someplace else, maybe we will consider that new immigrants coming into our country arrive for the same reasons as our ancestors. They also want a better life or a different life.

My grandfather, Rocco Liuzzi, arrived at Ellis Island from Montemurro, Italy in 1906. The area he was from is known as La Basilicata, and is about 120 miles southeast of Naples. Millions of people emigrated from Italy in the early 1900s, many of them single men who were farmers but would go on to be low-paid laborers in America. Rocco was an illiterate shepherd. In 1908, he returned home for a year because of high unemployment in America and married Mariantonia Mancini. He returned to America with his new wife in 1909. He worked for cousins as a rag picker in New York City. When they moved to Albany, New York a few years later, he first worked for his brother-in-law, who owned the Broadway Quick Shoe Repair, and then worked at the Albany Felt Company until retirement. In the sixty-two years he lived in America, Rocco and Mariantonia never learned to speak English, other than a few words. The Liuzzis had seven children, all born at home. One daughter, Carmela, would die at five years old from pneumonia. None of the five boys would graduate high school, because it was expected they would work as soon as they were able to help the family. Three of the brothers left school by ninth grade. Only my Aunt

Josephine would complete high school and attend Albany Business College to earn a secretarial certificate.

I can't speak directly to whether my grandparents felt isolated or discriminated against, since my grandmother died before I was born and my grandfather died when I was 11, but there was a lot of suspicion about Italian immigrants because such a large number emigrated between 1890 and 1920, the period known as the new immigration. The immigrants coming in this wave were mostly Jews, Slavs, and Italians. Old immigration immigrants were mostly British, Irish, Germans, and Scandinavians. Immigration laws passed in the 1920s attempted to change immigration patterns back to old immigration, with preferences for Northern Europeans.

My grandparents mostly lived in Italian neighborhoods and went to St. Anthony's (pronounced St. Ant-nees) in downtown Albany, a church my Aunt Josephine described as "an ethnic parish that served the Italian immigrants, and a lot of services were in Italian. All the Liuzzi siblings graduated eighth grade at St. Anthony's School."

When we visited my grandfather at Christmas and Easter each year until his death in 1968, we would sit quietly while my father spoke to his father in broken Italian—my father had forgotten most of his first spoken language since, like all the sons, he was out on the streets by seven years old selling newspapers or riding in the back of trucks as a jumper who helped unload cargo. I remember my aunt translating for her father and brother. She wrote and spoke Italian up until she died in 2005. The only English words I remember my grandfather speaking were when my father would ask, "How are you doing, Pops?" and my grandfather would respond, "Uh, I feel like a bum."

My father, Frank, was drafted to serve in World War II. He would meet my mother, Ruth, in Ryde, Australia, where he was stationed. My mother had dropped out of high school to work in order to help her mother, who became widowed at a young age with five children, losing her husband to complications from a chest injury sustained at Gallipoli in World War I—there is a photograph of him, taken in Gallipoli, carrying one of his wounded comrades on his shoulder to safety that is often printed in the news media on Anzac Day (a veteran's remembrance day for Australian and New Zealander soldiers similar to our Memorial Day and Veterans Day remembrances) in Australia.

After the war, Dad returned to Australia to marry my mother, and he worked there for a year at the same cut-glass factory at which she worked before they returned to Albany in 1946, and he got a job at Hamilton News and then Williams Press as a mailer. My mother was considered a "foreigner" because she was neither Italian nor Catholic, though she later converted to Catholicism. She was ostracized from the Liuzzi family for many years and felt isolated in her new country. Distance from her own family contributed to her deep loneliness. She would suffer depression and become an alcoholic.

Even though I had no intimate knowledge of the immigration of my grandparents and mother until I was older, I knew our family differed from many of the white, middle-class families of my fellow students at school. Growing up in a bicultural home ensured I always assessed other people with an open mind.

And when we look at the Dreamers, the children of undocumented workers who were brought here, often by corporations looking for cheap labor, as far back as the 1940s and 1950s, maybe we can look at them as we would our own children and accept them, rather than deport them to a country many of them don't even remember. They've paid taxes and fought wars for us. They deserve to be accepted in the country they know and love, and to know that their parents, many of whom have been here for dozens of years, will also be offered a path to citizenship. Maybe we will open our shores to refugees who only want to escape inhumane conditions and keep their families alive, safe, and together. When politicians like Trump call for America first, they are creating a baseless fear that helping others will mean fewer resources for us. We can afford to help and thrive.

Maybe we can acknowledge that some Americans have historically been subjugated and victims of genocide and remember that by pulling together, we can change the systems that allowed these heinous acts. Maybe we will acknowledge this chapter in our history for what it is: pages full of the names of black men, women, and children murdered at the hands of racially biased police officers, vigilantes, and terrorists, and the resurgence of white supremacy in mainstream culture.

One way to normalize the concept of an America of subcultures is to rely on the media to report it. The media are a pillar of our democracy. Its members must continue to fight the false news sites and the proliferation of alternative facts and find the truth. Journalists must question their biases, just like the rest of us.

We must also push for films, television programs, and commercials that reflect the demographics, subcultures, and regions of our country. Only then can we begin to know, understand, respect, and acknowledge that all Americans matter.

This country has room for everyone. There are enough resources, particularly if we stop the practice of corporations making large campaign donations that influence government representatives to consider corporate interests above the needs of their constituents. Most of us want the same things: a living-wage job, (or living-wage assistance for those who are unable to work), fair, affordable, and decent housing, safe neighborhoods with access to transportation, affordable, quality childcare, affordable groceries and goods stores, good schools, affordable health care, and short-term safety nets when life knocks us down.

It will never be perfect, but this grand country is a social experiment in which we must continue to work toward our ideals even if, like now, we fall far short of them. What we can't do is forget that individuals are affected in ways that can be catastrophic or fatal when we fail in our quest.

President Obama said it best in his speech in 2015 at the Edmund Pettus Bridge in Selma, Alabama, celebrating the 50th anniversary of the Civil Rights marches from Selma to Montgomery: "What greater expression of faith in the American experiment than this, what greater form of patriotism is there than the belief that America is not yet finished, that we are strong enough to be self-critical, that each successive generation can look upon our imperfections and decide that it is in our power to remake this nation to more closely align with our highest ideals?"

We must remember that every man, woman, or child assaulted or murdered by police officers, vigilantes, or domestic terrorists was a person just trying to live his life. They are the victims, not the bad people, and their lives mattered. Their families and friends are victims, too, left behind to mourn. They are children, and spouses, and siblings, and aunts, and uncles, and church members, and neighbors, and fathers, and mothers. We cannot heal the holes in their families' hearts and lives, but we can finally change the racial dynamic in America.

We can remember that most police officers are good citizens who have been called to serve their communities, while knowing that there are bad people everywhere, and we need to discover those who operate behind the veil of racial bias and make sure they are properly trained, disciplined when necessary, or routed from the police departments before someone is harmed or killed. We should do the same for those who represent us in the government. No one should hold elected or appointed positions of power, if he cannot serve all his constituents the same.

Most of all, we can no longer deny how harmful systemic racism and racial bias are now and have been. Take a look at the contrasts in Ronald's and my childhoods to illustrate the point.

I was the fourth of five children in our bicultural, working-class-poor home, all of us cramped into a 900-square-foot-house that my father paid for with a mortgage, in Colonie Village, a predominately white suburb located between Albany and Schenectady, New York. My mother's alcoholism and depression were both the source of daily frustrations and arguments between my parents, and bouts of neglect suffered especially by my youngest sibling and me. When I was 12 and my brother was 8, my father had a heart attack, and we lived on welfare and the kindness of neighbors who left food on our doorstep until the doctor cleared my father for work. I might have repeated the life my parents lived, one of economic struggle, low education, poverty, addiction, and sadness, except for teachers who nurtured my intelligence and creativity. Three of us became first-generation college graduates, and two of us have advanced degrees. I got to choose among three the college that offered the best scholarship and financial aid package. That is privilege. It may not seem so, but it is.

Ronald was also the fourth of five children. His parents, who married as teenagers, migrated from the South to Syracuse, New York, in the 1950s. They were strict parents. After living with relatives so they could get on their feet, they moved into an apartment in a Syracuse westside housing project. The residents of James-Geddes Housing were white, black, Hispanic, and Native American. The blocks of buildings still stand, though the residents may be even poorer than when Ronald's family lived there—a 2016 survey ranked Syracuse the 29th poorest city in the nation. They lived there until they could afford a house on the east side in a predominately Jewish middle-class neighborhood. Ronald was 12 when they moved, around the same time my family was collecting welfare. He remembers many of his teachers as dismissive, telling him "Too bad you come from a broken family," even though he didn't, and "You will never go to college," although he did. Others were apologetic, perhaps because they recognized he was intelligent and creative, too, but they assumed he would never reach his potential. He and one other sibling became first-generation college graduates. He was admitted to Syracuse University because he walked to the administration building with his art portfolio and told them he wanted to go to college. His guidance counselor, unlike mine, who invited me to one college recruitment session after another, never talked to him about college. Had Ronald lacked chutzpah to walk up to a major private university and ask for admission, he may never have attended college, nor met me, for that matter, during freshman year at Syracuse University.

I still have hope, no matter how dark the days become under a Trump administration. I know hope keeps the Mothers of the Movement out in the public eye, sharing their stories, hoping that America will come to know that their sons' and daughters' lives mattered. As I explained in chapter nineteen, when I recall most things are temporary, no matter how bad they get, I can usually get to the other side of them. I know we can get to the other side of this.

One day, I hope that Ronald and I are just another aging couple. That our daughters are just women living their lives, not worried about being judged by the color of their skin or by their gender. That boys like Trayvon Martin, Tamir Rice, Darius Simmons, Jordan Davis, and Jordan Edwards can walk home in the rain, or play in the park, or listen to music in a car, because they belong right where they are, and no one questions why they are there, or calls the police, or pulls a gun. That women like Sandra Bland can drive across country and start a new job. That men like Michael Brown, Freddie Gray, Terence Crutcher, Keith Lamont Scott, Alton Sterling, and Philando Castile can live their lives without constant police attention that may escalate and end in death. That men like Timothy Caughman and Richard Collins III can walk on the street or stand at the bus stop and not worry that some white supremacist will pick them at random to make a hateful point. That pastors like Clementa Pinckney can lead a fellowship service for his faithful parishioners, invite a stranger to join them in prayer, and know it will be okay, because his faith tells him so. That men like Kalvin Michael Smith will never have to serve prison time for crimes they didn't commit. That police officers who engage in misconduct, excessive force, and racial bias lose their jobs at the very least, and get convicted and serve prison time if they commit assault or murder. That communities can rely on and trust the police to protect and serve their residents. That a man like Barack Obama or a woman like Hillary Clinton can be elected to the highest office in the land and fulfill their responsibilities without obstruction, interference, nor the cloud of racism or misogyny hanging over their every action. That we elect a president who knows how to unite us, empower us to fulfill our civic duties, and who cares about the welfare of all Americans, not just the few who hold all the wealth. That journalists report about how well community policing is working, instead of how many black men, women, and children have been murdered at the hands of police, vigilantes, and white supremacists. That the doors of the

Mothers of the Movement club close to new members, because there are no new members to be had.

Only then will we know what post-racialism looks like in America.

Only then will we stop shouting, "black lives matter," or taking a knee during the anthem, or posting "just another day" racially motivated incidents on Facebook. It won't be just another day. It will be a new day in America, because America will have risen to its greatest ideal: the ideal that we are all created equal.

Discussion Questions for Classrooms and Book Clubs

Thank you for reading this book. I know it was emotional. Conversations about race can be volatile and jarring. It is the reason most people dislike talking about race, to the point of ignoring race altogether, no matter what is happening in our country. For your discussion, pledge to make the gathering a safe space where no one is attacked for being honest, and every question or comment will be respectfully examined and discussed. The most important role for every participant is that of listener. Have an open mind—that means being willing to let go of some of your beliefs and being open to learning about a different perspective. Remember, empathy, the ability to understand and share another's feelings, is important in understanding another perspective that does not match yours. It is okay if people come to the conversation with old paradigms and beliefs still strongly held. These kinds of conversations can change minds and create allies in the effort to change the race narrative in America.

1) What do you think the title means?
2) What were some of the emotions you felt as you read the book? Why do you think you felt that way?
3) Did this book affect the way in which you think about race? In what ways?
4) Which of the many stories in the book had the biggest impact on you? Why?
5) How old were you and what is your first memory of learning about race? How does that memory make you feel now? Did it help shape your beliefs about race?
6) Based on what you learned in the book, how would you define the following words? Are the words

negative, positive, neutral or all three? How do the definitions differ from what you thought the definitions were before you read the book?

- Bias
- Racism
- Stereotype
- Ethnic
- Colorblind
- Privilege
- Post-racial
- Racist
- Nationalism
- White supremacy
- Black militant
- Excessive use of force
- Systemic racism/Institutional racism

7) What legacy of slavery and racial oppression from our history do you see in our country today?

8) Where do you draw your beliefs about race today? Television, news media, social media, personal experience, or all of the above? How do they shape your beliefs about race? Are they positive or negative influences?

9) In what ways do you think you have internalized stereotypes about race? Explore which stereotypes inform your beliefs about race. Which ones do you think are the most harmful to yourself or to members of the race about which the beliefs are held?

10) What stereotypes exist about the race you identify with? How do you feel when people rely on them to judge your character and form an opinion about you? What have you done to personally dismantle the power of stereotypes?

11) Have you ever been pulled over by the police? What was the experience like? How does it compare to the police stops discussed in this book?

12) Have you ever been in a situation where someone of a different race made you feel uncomfortable or afraid? Why? How did you handle the situation?

13) Have you ever talked about race with people of your own race? With people of a different race? How did those conversations compare? Why?

14) Have you ever been hurt by someone who said something racially insensitive? How did you handle the situation?

15) Have you ever been accused of saying something racially insensitive? How did you handle the situation?

16) Have you ever witnessed someone saying or doing something racially insensitive to another person? How did you handle the situation?

17) Do you have work colleagues, neighbors, classmates, friends, church members, or family who are a different race than you? If you don't, why do you think that is? How do you feel about them? How do you think they feel about you? Have you had conversations about race? Were the conversations negative or positive?

18) Recall the most recent news story you read or viewed about race. What was your reaction to it? Talk about how the story was covered.

19) Can you think of ways in which racism is systemic in the United States? Institutional?

20) How can we change institutional and systemic racism? What can you do personally to help bring about change?

21) What do you pledge today to do differently in terms of how you engage with people of a different race, talk about race, or acknowledge racism?

Acknowledgements

"A good editor doesn't rewrite words, she rewires synapses."
~ S. Kelley Harrell

A writer can have a way with words, tell a compelling and evocative narrative, pour her physical, mental, and emotional energy into creating the work, but an editor is the one who offers support and guidance, and who challenges the writer to dig deeper or stop preaching or get to the real story that needs to be told. Like a professional baker considering a new recipe, she is the one who reviews the manuscript for accuracy, proper flavoring, and the right consistency, and determines if it is complete, like the baker who pokes the toothpick in the cake in the oven to see if it is done. When readers are deciding what they want to read next, the editor knows how to serve up a manuscript for consumption.

I've been fortunate to have two editors work on this book: one who has known me for over fifty years, and the other for eight.

I met Rosemary Armao when I was nine and she and my oldest brother started dating in high school. They would be married for thirty-five years before divorcing. In that time she became a journalist, editor, and educator, known across the world for teaching young journalists about investigative reporting. She met my childhood oral narratives, emoted and enacted with passion, facial expressions, voice changes, and vigorous hand movements, as if they were the best she'd ever heard, and when I wrote my first short memoir many years ago, she told me my story was important to share, but that I needed to show the story, and not just tell it. She recommended a few books to help the process. I read them, wrote sometimes and not others while working and raising children, and had a couple of articles published. Then I decided I wanted to get better at telling my stories.

At age fifty I applied to the MFA program at Queens University of Charlotte. It would be my second master's degree. I had finished the first one in professional education studies two years before, a degree I started immediately after my twin daughters left home to attend a dance conservatory their senior year of high school. I met Lacey Lyons on the first day of school at Queens. I wore my anxiety like a scratchy sweater, worried I was too old, couldn't handle full-time school while also working full time, or that I was not a good enough writer to be there, but Lacey was a welcoming, calm face in the crowd, and I instantly took to her. She also has a degree in journalism and she not only teaches writing at her undergrad alma mater, but also is an advocate for people with disabilities, gaining recognition across her home state of Tennessee for her contributions in the field. Our friendship grew over the two-year program, and when we graduated, I recommended her to edit a project to which some of us new graduates had committed – an anthology on race and culture written by a diverse group of women, a book that sadly will not be published.

Both Lacey and Rosemary edited my essays for the anthology. I knew when I wanted to write this book that I wanted their input, because this book needed to be respectful, compassionate, and authentic. Both know my passion for equality and justice. Both understand my sense of urgency in sharing my stories about what I experience as a white woman married to a black man, and as a woman who raised mixed-race twin daughters. Both are sharp editors who challenge me to tell my stories better and hold me to it. I appreciated every comment, added comma, and deleted word during this process, even the ones that made my stomach tighten or the back of my neck grow warm with frustration. Each time, I dove back in for another revision. This cake is done.

Another Queens University MFA graduate pushed me to self-publish. Melissa Prunty Kemp and I didn't meet at school. We met via social media after we graduated. We spent many a late night messaging about race in America, sharing experiences and often, frustration, anger, depression, and hopelessness. When I contacted her about this book, she said, "It's about time!" I knew then I had to complete it.

I grew up in an inter-ethnic family. My father was first-generation American-born Italian. His father arrived on US shores in 1906. He returned to Italy in 1908, and brought a wife back to America with him in 1909. My father learned to speak English when he started school. His parents never mastered English. My mother was a World War II war bride from Australia. They met while my father was stationed there. Neither of my parents graduated high school, but both were intelligent, empathetic, and insightful. My childhood was difficult at times, as many childhoods are, since there were five children and my dad's job in the mailroom of a printing press business barely earned enough to feed and shelter us. We were working-class poor, and, at one point, when my dad suffered a heart attack when I was twelve, we lived on welfare and the kindness of neighbors, who left food on our doorstep for a few months while he recovered. My mother was bored by housework and raising five children in such a small house, isolated from family thousands of miles away in Australia, and ostracized by my father's family for being a foreigner. She suffered depression and became an alcoholic. But my parents were unique, maybe because we lived a bicultural life. They were open to others who were different from their ethnic, cultural, political, and religious experiences. My father's best friend was the grandson of slaves. I knew what homosexuality was by age nine because a gay couple lived up the street and my parents befriended them, while other neighbors avoided them. Older siblings' college friends would come visit for the weekend, and they came from all over, as far away as Kenya, worrying friends and neighbors alike. Neighbors thought we were eccentric, but such an upbringing ensured I would look at people as individuals. That openness allowed me to see Ronald, my husband, for the person he is, not as a dermatological mass, perceived through bias and stereotypes. Sadly, my parents would not get to know him. Their liberal perspective ended when it came to their youngest daughter. We didn't speak for some years over my relationship with Ronald. By that time, my mother was in advanced stages of alcoholism, and I believe her state contributed to her harsh reaction and my father's reaction in turn, a strong rejection I had not anticipated, given all they'd taught us. Then they each passed away, eighteen months apart, just as they were beginning to come around and we were trying to repair our broken relationship. In spite of our several years of estrangement, they taught me every person deserves to be treated with respect, fairness, and without prejudice. I thank them for giving me that valuable lesson. My life is full because of it.

My twin daughters, Cara and Mackenzie, have shown me how to live in that space where races intersect with grace, humor, intelligence, outspokenness, and artistic expression. We had to speak about race for the first time when they were three. We had hoped to wait a few years longer, but black families talk to their children about race very early on. It is a necessary conversation, often prompted by interactions with others. In this case, their day care teacher had brought it up in a lesson on ethnicity. She told us when we picked them up, and she was visibly uncomfortable about it. When we got home, Mackenzie asked Ronald, "Are you black?"

"Yes, I'm black."

"Is Mama black, too?"

"No, Mama is white."

"Then I'm white, too," she said, stamping her foot, arms crossed.

All our discussions about race over the years taught me so much, and also made me want to write this book. I still hope for a better world for them, even though, as adults, they have their own power to change the world.

I married my soul mate when I married Ronald, but I would learn later that I married my hero, too. When we met freshman year of college, I only knew he was an art major with a minor in music and that he played percussion in a rhythm and blues band. As we started our journey together, and I began my own journey of learning about race in America, I discovered other wonderful things about him, too, like his strong need to be of service to others, in spite of how he is treated as a black man in America. That calling led him to be one of the first black firefighters on his department, and the third black officer in department history. I still feel the effect such trailblazing had on his mind and emotions. Unlike the physical scars he received fighting fires, these scars are invisible to others, but I see them clearly.

His strong support of my writing and the telling of our stories helped me to stay focused and motivated, even those times when he declined to read my essays, saying they elicited too much pain. I believe him. When he read my memoir, my MFA thesis, he said it made him cry because he felt I understood him and what he experienced. I also appreciate his patience while I continue to learn about race and racism in America. Forty-three years is not long enough to understand the complexity of race relations, which span over 400 years of our country's history. He understands why I still react with outrage about racially motivated incidents that personally affect us, or that we see in the news, while he has always known about them and expects such things to happen, and, while not accepting of them, neither is he surprised.

I am thankful to all the people who crossed my path in sixty-some years, those who opened my mind and helped me see beyond my own perspective, and especially those who showed me strength and hope in the face of unprecedented prejudice, violence, and discrimination, when the rest of us would have run for cover. In spite of a disingenuous message from the far right about the free things people hope to get for having brown skin and for those who live in poverty, I know that is not the case. People of color and those living in poverty know nothing in life is free; especially equality, and they are prepared to fight for it. I add my voice to theirs.

Bibliography

Dedication
Funke, Daniel and Tina Susman. "From Ferguson to Baton Rouge: Deaths of black men and women at the hands of police." *LATimes.com*. Los Angeles Times, 12 Jul. 2016. Web. 22 Aug. 2017.

Introduction
Associated Press. "AP Poll: U.S. majority have prejudice against blacks." *Usatoday.com*. USA Today, 27 Oct. 2012. Web. 23 Aug. 2017.

"Death of Jonny Gammage." *Wikipedia*, Wikimedia Foundation, 2 Mar. 2017, En.wikipedia.org/wiki/Death_of_Jonny_Gammage.

"Death of Sandra Bland." *Wikipedia*, Wikimedia Foundation, 22 Aug. 2017, en.wikipedia.org/wiki/Death_of_Sandra_Bland

"Emmett Till." *Wikipedia*, Wikimedia Foundation, 21 Aug.2017, en.wikipedia.org/wiki/Emmett_Till

"Emmett Till murderers make magazine confession." *This Day in History*. The History Channel. 24 Jan. 2016. Web. 24 Aug. 2017.

Gruson, Lindsey. "Syracuse Grapples With Debate Over Civilian Review of Police." *Nytimes.com*. The New York Times, 3 Aug. 1992. Web. 23 Aug. 2017.

Harwood, Matthew. "How Did America's Police Get So Militarized?" *Motherjones.com*. Mother Jones. 14 Aug. 2014. Web. 23 Aug. 2017.

Haugh, Christopher. "How the Dallas Police Department Reformed Itself." *TheAtlantic.com*. Atlantic Media, Inc., 9 Jul. 2016. Web. 24 Aug. 2017.

Mitchell, Jerry. "Emmett Till's accuser admits she lied. What now?." *Usatoday.com.* USA Today, 7 Feb.2017. Web. 24 Aug. 2017.

Sebastian, Michael. "Who Are the 'Mothers of the Movement' Speaking at the Democratic National Convention?" *Elle.com.* Hearst Magazines, 26 Jul. 2016. Web. 23 Aug. 2017.

Staff Reports. "Location changed for Clinton campaign event that will include mothers of Trayvon Martin, Sandra Bland in Winston-Salem." *Journalnow.com.* Winston-Salem Journal, 21 Oct. 2016. Web. 23 Aug. 2017.

"The death of Emmett Till." *This Day in History.* The History Channel. 28 Aug. 2016.

Web. 23 Aug. 2017.

Chapter 1: Profiling Fatality
Robertson, Campbell and John Schwartz. "Shooting Focuses Attention on a Program That Seeks to Avoid Guns." *Nytimes.com.* The New York Times, 22 Mar. 2012. Web. 24 Aug. 2017.

Chapter 2: Profiling Fatality 2: More on Trayvon Martin
"Video shows white teens driving over, killing black man, says DA." AC 360. Drew Griffin and Scott Bronstein. CNN. 8 Aug. 2011. *Cnn.com.* Web. 30 Aug. 2017.

Chapter 3: Profiling Fatality 3: The Demonization of George Zimmerman
Capehart, Jonathan. "George Zimmerman goes gun shopping." *Washingtonpost.com.* The Washington Post, 26 Aug. 2013. Web. 30 Aug. 2017.

Crugnale, James. "Gun Groups Seek to Fund George Zimmerman's Defense." *Mediaite*. Abrams Media Network, 2 Apr. 2012. Web. 30 Aug. 2017.

"George Zimmerman." *Wikipedia*, Wikimedia Foundation, 28 Aug. 2017. En.wikipedia.org/wiki/George_Zimmerman.

Chapter 6: Diminishing Racism, One Granite Countertop at a Time

Bowerman, Mary. "Black women kicked off Napa Valley Wine Train settle." *Usatoday.com*. USA Today, 20 Apr. 2016. Web. 1 Sept. 2017.

Cohen, Andrew. "Racial Bias in Death Penalty Cases: A North Carolina Test." *TheAtlantic.com*. Atlantic Media, Inc., 23 Apr. 2012. Web. 30 Aug. 2017.

Gardner, Eriq. "ABC's 'The Bachelor' to Be Sued for Racial Discrimination." *Hollywoodreporter.com*. The Hollywood Reporter, 17 Apr. 2012. Web. 30 Aug. 2017.

Hillin, Taryn. "People Are Already Being Racist Toward Rachel, the First Black 'Bachelorette.'"

Entitymag.com. Entity, 15 Feb. 2017. Web. 1 Sept. 2017.

"North Carolina Racial Justice Act Ruling Summary." *North Carolina Racial Justice Act Ruling Summary:*

Death Penalty Information Center. Death Penalty Information Center, www.deathpenaltyinfo.org/north-carolina-racial-justice-act-ruling-summary

"Nielsen Estimates 116.4 Million TV Homes In The U.S. For The 2015-16 TV Season." *Nielson.com*.

Nielson, 28 Aug. 2015. Web. 1 Sept. 2017.

Otterson, Joe. "TV Ratings: 'The Bachelorette' Season 13 Premiere Holds Solid on ABC." *Variety.com*

Variety, 23 May 2017. Web. 1 Sept. 2017.

"Rachel Lindsay Will Debut As The First Black 'Bachelorette.'" *Morning Edition.* Narr. David Greene. NPR. 22 May 2017. Web. 1 Sept. 2017.

Raine, Lee and D'Vera Cohn. "Census: Computer ownership, internet connection varies widely across U.S." *Pewresearch.org.* Pew Research Center, 19 Sept. 2014. Web. 31 Aug. 2017.

Schoellkopf, Christina. "How 'The Bachelorette' Picked the Men for Rachel's Historic Season." *Hollywoodreporter.com.* The Hollywood Reporter, 19 May 2017. Web. 1 Sept. 2017.

"Supreme Court Declares Same-Sex Marriage Legal In All 50 States." *The Two-Way.* Narr. Bill Chappell. NPR. 26 Jun. 2015. Web. 1 Sept. 2017.

Victor, Daniel. "Ouster of 'Disruptive' Book Club From Napa Train Prompts Racial Bias Charge." *Nytimes.com.* The New York Times, 24 Aug. 2015. Web. 1 Sept. 2017.

Chapter 7: The Door of No Return

Cobb, Jelani. "Rachel Jeantel on Trial." *Newyorker.com.* Conde Nast, 27 Jun. 2013. Web. 1 Sept. 2017.

Dalesio, Emery P. and Jonathan Drew. "Ballot Fraud Scandal: Criminal charges filed against political operative Leslie McCrae Dowless Jr in undecided N. Carolina congressional race." *The Ledger.* 27 Feb. 2019.

Greenwood, Max and Rachel Frazin. "GOP's Mark Harris won't run again in contested North Carolina House race." TheHill.com. The Hill, 26 Feb. 2019

Liptak, Adam. "Justices Reject 2 Gerrymandered North Carolina Districts, Citing Racial Bias."*Nytimes.com.* The New York Times, 22 May 2017. Web. 2 Sept. 2017.

Specht, Paul. "NC GOP Misleads about NC Election Fraud Investigation." *www.politifact.com*. Politifact NC, 4 Dec 2018.

Terkel, Amanda. "Ben Carson: Slaves Were Immigrants Who Came Here And Worked Really Hard 'For Less.'" *Huffingtonpost.com*. The Huffington Post, 6 Mar. 2017. Web. 2 Sept. 2017.

Thompson, Krissah and Lonnae O'Neal Parker. "For Trayvon Martin's friend Rachel Jeantel, a 'village' of mentors trying to keep her on track." *Washingtonpost.com*. The Washington Post, 4 Jun. 2014. Web. 2 Sept. 2017.

Chapter 8: To Trayvon, With Love

Jealous, Benjamin Todd. "Justice Department: Open a Civil Rights Case Against George Zimmerman." *MoveOn.org*. Web. 2 Sept. 2017.

Pantazi, Andrew. "Michael Dunn gets life, plus 90 years for Jordan Davis killing." *Jacksonville.com*. The Florida Times-Union, 23 Feb. 2017. Web. 2 Sept. 2017.

Chapter 9: Outraged

Cox, John Woodrow. "'We're going to put a bullet in your head:' #PizzaGate threats terrorize D.C. shop Owners." *Washingtonpost.com*. The Washington Post, 6 Dec. 2016. Web. 2 Sept. 2017.

Villines, Zawn. "Did the Abortion Rate Drop Because of Obamacare?" *DailyKos*. Kos Media, LLC, 19 Jan. 2017. Web. 2 Sept. 2017.

Chapter 10: Biased Much?

Associated Press. "Neighbor, 76, sentenced to life without parole for shooting dead unarmed black 13-year-old." *Dailymail.co.uk*. The Daily Mail, 22 Jul. 2013. Web. 5 Sept. 2017.

Eligon, John. "In Missouri, Race Complicates a Transfer to Better Schools." *Nytimes.com*. The New York Times, 31 Jul. 2013. Web. 5 Sept. 2017.

Kunapuli, Deepa. "50 Years Ago, A Legendary Writer Asked A Very Simple Question About The World We Live In." *Upworthy*. Cloud Tiger Media, Inc., 30 Jul. 2013. Web. 5 Sept. 2017.

"Renee Vaughn holds a sign as the G. Zimmerman River Oaks Stand Your Ground group holds a counter demonstration." 2017. The Associated Press. JPEG file.

Stanley-Becker, Isaac. "Darius Simmons' mother describes watching John Spooner gun down son." *Archive.jsonline.com*. The Milwaukie-Wisconsin Journal Sentinel, 17 Jul.2013. Web. 6 Sept. 2017.

Chapter 13: This is What Apartheid Looks Like in America

Black Lives Matter. Home page. Black Lives Matter, 2017. Web. 10 Sept. 2017.

Clarke, Rachel and Mariano Castillo. "Michael Brown shooting: What Darren Wilson told the Ferguson grand jury." *Cnn.com*. CNN, 26 Nov. 2014. Web. 6 Sept. 2017.

"DOJ clears Darren Wilson in Michael Brown killing." *CBS News*. CBS, 4 Mar. 2015. *Cbsnews.com*. Web. 14 Sept. 2017.

Ferrise, Adam. "Tamir Rice 911 call-taker suspended." *Cleveland.com*. Cleveland.com, 15 Mar. 2017. Web. 10 Sept. 2017.

Hanna, Jason and Amanda Watts. "Tamir Tice shooting probe: 1 officer fired, 1 suspended." *Cnn.com*. CNN, 30 May 2017. Web. 14 Sept. 2017.

Johnson, Walter. "Ferguson's Fortune 500 Company." *The Atlantic.com*. Atlantic Media, Inc., 26 Apr. 2015. Web. 10 Sept. 2017.

King, Shaun. "The outrageous and tragic hiring of officer Timothy Loehmann by the Cleveland police." *Daily Kos*. Kos Media, LLC, 9 Jan. 2015. Web. 14 Sept. 2017.

Chapter 14: Long, Cold Winter of Justice
"Birmingham Church Bombing." *This Day in History*. The History Channel. 15 Sept. 2010. Web. 14 Sept. 2017.

Chapter 15: Sleeting Justice
"2015 Clinton Correctional Facility escape." *Wikipedia*, Wikimedia Foundation, 14 Sept. 2017, En.wikipedia.org/wiki/2015_Clinton_Correctional_Facility _escape.

"Escaped N. Carolina convict back in custody." *CBS News*. CBS, 29 Jun. 2015. *Cbsnews.com*. Web. 14 Sept. 2017.

Stanglin, Doug and Michael Winter. "Chapel Hill 'rocked' by killings of 3 Muslim students."

Usatoday.com. USA Today, 11 Feb. 2015. Web. 14 Sept. 2017.

Chapter 16: No More
Adler-Bell, Sam. "America's white fragility complex: Why white people get so defensive about their privilege." *Salon.com*. Salon Media Group, 17 Mar. 2015. Web. 20 Sept. 2017.

Associated Press. "Dylann Roof ruled competent to stand trial." *Nypost.com*. New York Post, 25 Nov. 2016. Web. 20 Sept. 2017.

Callahan, Yesha. "DeAndre Harris' Attorney Speaks Out About Charges, Says White Supremacist Was Hit by

Someone Else." *The Root.* Gizmodo Media Group, 11 Oct. 2017. Web. 25 Oct. 2017.

Crews, Donald. "True Nazis." Letter. *Winston-Salem Journal* 11 Sept. 2017. Web. 25 Oct. 2017.

Green, Jordan. "Meet Harold Ray Crews, the Main Street White Nationalist." *Triad City Beat.* Web. 5 Dec. 2017.

Hatewatch Staff. "Meet the League: State Chairmen and Organizers of the League of the South." *Splcenter.org.* The Southern Poverty Law Center, 9 Aug. 2017. Web. 25 Oct. 2017.

Hauser, Christine. "DeAndre Harris, Beaten by White Supremacists in Charlottesville, Is Found Not Guilty of Assault." *Nytimes.com* New York Times, 16 Mar. 2018.

Hill, Michael. Harold Crews injury photo. League of the South Web. 11 Oct. 2017.

Hinton, John. "Walkertown man gets arrest warrant for unlawful wounding against man beaten in Charlottesville unrest." *Journalnow.com.* Winston-Salem Journal, 23 Oct. 2017. Web. 25 Oct. 2017.

Jarvie, Jenny. "A video of his beating by white nationalists in Charlottesville went viral. Now he is among those facing arrest." *Latimes.com.* Los Angeles Times, 11 Oct. 2017. Web. 25 Oct. 2017.

Lee, Trymaine. "Man Attacked in Charlottesville Charged With Assault in Unexpected Turn." *Nbcnews.com.* NBC, 10 Oct. 2017. Web. 25 Oct. 2017.

Mele, Christopher. "New Orleans Begins Removing Confederate Monuments, Under Police Guard." *Nytimes.com.* The New York Times, 24 Apr. 2017. Web. 20 Sept. 2017.

Shapira, Ian and Derek Hawkins. "Black man attacked by white supremacists in Charlottesville faces felony charge." *Washingtonpost.com.* The Washington Post, 11 Oct. 2017. Web. 25 Oct. 2017.

Wilson, Patrick. "Gov. McAuliffe wants arrests in beating of man in Charlottesville during white supremacist violence." *Richmond.com*. Richmond Times-Dispatch, 21 Aug. 2017. Web. 20 Sept. 2017.

Chapter 17: #AltonSterling #PhilandoCastile

Grant, Richard. "The True Story of the 'Free State of Jones.'" *Smithsonianmag.com*. Smithsonian Institution, Mar. 2016. Web. 23 Sept. 2017.

Holliday, Billie. "Strange Fruit." *Lady Sings the Blues*. Azlyrics.com, 2017.

Lewis, Danny. "This Map Shows Over a Century of Documented Lynchings in the United States." *Smithsonianmag.com*. Smithsonian Institution, 24 Jan. 2017. Web. 23 Sept. 2017.

Ockerman, Emma. "Read the Transcript of the Video Taken During Philando Castile Shooting in Minnesota." *Time.com*. Time, Inc., 7 Jul. 2016. Web. 23 Sept. 2017.

Park, Madison. "The 62-second encounter between Philando Castile and the officer who killed him." *Cnn.com*. CNN, 30 May 2017. Web. 23 Sept. 2017.

"Shooting of Alton Sterling." *Wikipedia*, Wikimedia Foundation, 23 Sept. 2017, En.wikipedia.org/wiki/Shooting_of_Alton_Sterling.

Smith, Mitch. "Minnesota Officer Acquitted in Killing of Philando Castile." *Nytimes.com*. The New York Times, 16 Jun. 2017. Web. 23 Sept. 2017.

"Strange Fruit." *Wikipedia*, Wikimedia Foundation, 23 Sept. 2017, En.wikipedia.org/wiki/Strange_Fruit.

Steinbuch, Yaron and Joe Tacopino. "Woman records horrific scene after boyfriend is fatally shot by police." *Nypost.com*. New York Post, 7 July 2016. Web. 23 Sept. 2017.

Chapter 18: America Broke My Spirit

"Former KKK Leader David Duke Says 'Of Course' Trump Voters Are His Voters." *The Two-Way.* Narr. Camila Domonoske. NPR, 5 Aug. 2016. *Npr.org.* Web. 27 Sept. 2017.

Hanson, Hilary. "Ex-KKK Leader David Duke Says White Supremacists Will 'Fulfill' Trump's Promises."

Huffingtonpost.com. The Huffington Post, 12 Aug. 2017. Web. 28 Sept. 2017.

Hatewatch Staff. "Edging closer to militancy, the neo-Confederate League of the South says it's forming a force to combat the 'leftist menace to our historic Christian civilization.'" *Splcenter.org.* The Southern Poverty Law Center, 6 Feb. 2017. Web. 27 Sept. 2017.

Hatewatch Staff. "League of the South Announces Formation of 'Southern Defense Force.'"

Splcenter.org. The Southern Poverty Law Center, 6 Feb. 2017. Web. 28 Sept. 2017.

Hill, Michael. "The Poison of Multiculturalism." *Dixienet.org.* The League of the South, 26 Sept. 2017. Web. 26 Sept. 2017.

Killian, Joe. "Bill eliminating concealed carry gun permits moves forward." *The Progressive Pulse.* NC Policy Watch. 31 May 2017. Web. 28 Sept. 2017.

Lowery, Wesley, Renae Merle, and Mark Berman. "Video shot by Keith Lamont Scott's wife shows her pleading with officers for his life." *Washingtonpost.com.* The Washington Post, 23 Sept. 2016. Web. 28 Sept. 2017.

Montanaro, Domenico. "Hillary Clinton's 'Basket of Deplorables,' In Full Context of This Ugly Campaign."

Npr.org. National Public Radio, 10 Sept. 2016. Web. 26 Sept. 2017.

"Ohio Trump campaign chair Kathy Miller says there was 'no racism' before Obama." *Theguardian.com.* The Guardian, 22 Sept. 2016. Web. 27 Sept. 2017.

"Tulsa Police Officer Is Found Not Guilty In Death of Terence Crutcher." *The Two-Way*. Narr. Bill Chappell. NPR, 18 May 2017. Web. 28 Sept. 2017.

Yan, Holly, Rolando Zenteno, and Brian Todd. "Keith Scott killing: No charge against officer." *Cnn.com*. CNN, 30 Nov. 2016. Web. 28 Sept. 2017.

Youngman, Clayton. "Tiffany Crutcher says Shelby trial showed 'corruption' of TPD, asks jury for justice."

Ktul.com. ABC Tulsa, 17 May 2017. Web. 28 Sept. 2017.

Chapter 19: I Am Tired of Talking about Race and Gender, Too

Bacon, John. "Law Center: Hate crime activity has declined since election." *Usatoday.com*. USA Today, 5 Jan. 2017. Web. 30 Sept. 2017.

Ekins, Emily. "Policing in America: Understanding Public Attitudes Toward the Police. Results from a National Survey." *Cato.org*. The Cato Institute, 7 Dec. 2016. Web. 30 Sept. 2017.

"Heroism or Terrorism?." *Snopes.com*.Snopes.com, n.d. Web. 30 Sept. 2017.

Pavascandola, Rocco and Larry McShane. "Exclusive: Rutgers University professor taken for psych evaluation after 'threatening' gun control, flag burning tweets." *Nydailynews.com*. New York Daily News, 16 Nov. 2016. Web. 30 Sept. 2017.

Pickens, Josie. "The Destruction of Black Wall Street." *Ebony*. Ebony Media Operations, 31 May 2013. Web. 30 Sept. 2017.

Tanenbaum, Michael. "Rutgers professor forced into psych evaluation over Second Amendment

tweets." *Phillyvoice.com*. WWB Holdings, LLC, 17 Nov. 2016. Web. 30 Sept. 2017.

Chapter 20: Countdown to 2020

Khullar, Dhruv. "How Prejudice Can Harm Your Health." *Nytimes.com*. The New York Times, 8 Jun. 2017. Web. 2 Oct. 2017.

"Poverty." *The State of Working America*. Economic Policy Institute, n.d. Web. 2 Oct. 2017.

Chapter 21: Not the Last Chapter

Associated Press. "Murder of Bowie State Student May Have Been Hate Crime." *Usnews.com*. U.S. News and World Report, 22 May 2017. Web. 9 Oct. 2017.

Biekiempis, Victoria. "Parents of racist killer James Jackson to stop paying for lawyer; judge will appoint defense for Timothy Caughman's murderer." *Nydailynews.com*. New York Daily News, 3 Apr. 2017. Web. 5 Oct. 2017.

Berube, Alan and Brad McDearman. "Good fortune, dire poverty, and inequality in Baltimore: An American story." *The Avenue*. The Brookings Institution, 11 May 2015. Web. 5 Oct. 2017.

Brennan, Christopher. "KKK leader says that he is 'glad' about Heather Heyer's death."

Nydailynews.com. New York Daily News, 15 Aug. 2017. Web. 11 Oct. 2017.

Brice-Saddler, Michael and Berman, Mark. "White supremacist pleads guilty to killing a black man with a sword in New York. *Washingtonpost.com*. Washington Post, 23 Jan. 2019.

Burns, Sarah. "Why Trump Doubled Down on the Central Park Five." *Nytimes.com*. The New York Times, 17 Oct. 2016. Web. 10 Oct. 2017.

"Darryl Hunt." *The Innocence Project*. The Innocence Project, n.d. Web. 5 Oct. 2017.

Dienst, Jonathan. "White Supremacist in NYC Sword Killing Charged With Murder as Terrorism."
        Nbcnewyork.com. NBC, 24 Mar. 2017. Web. 3 Oct. 2017.

Downs, Kenya. "When black death goes viral, it can trigger PTSD-like trauma." *The Rundown*. PBS Newshour, 22 Jul. 2016. Web. 3 Oct. 2017.

Fenton, Justin. "Baltimore Police Officer Alicia White, charged in Freddie Gray case, becomes the first to speak out." *Baltimoresun.com*. The Baltimore Sun, 17 Nov. 2016. Web. 5 Oct. 2017.

Fitzsimmons, Emma G. "Key to Improving Subway Service in New York? Modern Signals." *Nytimes.com*. The New York Times, 1 May 2017. Web. 11 Oct. 2017.

"Freddie Gray's death in police custody-what we know." *Bbc.com*. BBC News, 23 May 2016. Web. 5 Oct. 2017.

George, Cindy. "Do You Have Post-Traumatic Slave Syndrome?." *Ebony*. Ebony Media Operations, 26 Aug. 2015. Web. 2 Oct. 2017.

Green, Emma. "Why the Charlottesville Marchers Were Obsessed With Jews." *The Atlantic*. Atlantic Media, Inc., 15 Aug. 2017. Web. 11 Oct. 2017.

Greene, Leonard. "President Trump's Twitter silence on Timothy Caughman's murder by white Supremacists speaks volumes." *Nydailynews.com*. New York Daily News, 23 Mar. 2017. Web. 7 Oct. 2017.

Hamilton, Megan. "Studies Conclude: Majority of Trump Voters Motivated By Racism-Not Just Economic Concerns." *Reverb Press*. Reverb Press, 7 Apr. 2017. Web. 7 Oct. 2017.

Hewlett, Michael. "Kalvin Michael Smith is out of prison but he's still not free." *Journalnow.com*. Winston-Salem Journal, 4 Jun. 2017. Web. 9 Oct. 2017.

Jones, Sarah. "Trump Goes On Racist Rant, Says Peacefully Protesting Black NFL Players Scare People." *Politics USA.* Politics USA, 28 Sept. 2017. Web. 11 Oct. 2017.

Lange, Jeva. "Donald Trump's 30-year crusade against the Central Park Five." *The Week.* The Week, 7 Oct. 2016. Web. 9 Oct. 2017.

Lapowsky, Issie. "A Campus Murder Tests Facebook Clicks As Evidence of Hate." *Wired.* Conde Nast, 23 May 2017. Web. 9 Oct. 2017.

Megerian, Chris. "What Donald Trump has said through the years about where President Obama was born." *Latimes.com.* Los Angeles Times, 16 Sept. 2016. Web. 10 Oct. 2017.

Mindock, Clark. "Taking a knee: Why are NFL players protesting and when did they start to kneel?." *Independent.co.uk.* The Independent, 25 Sept. 2017. Web. 11 Oct. 2017.

Molnar, Alexandra. "From Europe to America: Immigration Through Family Tales." *Mtholyoke.edu.* 15 Dec. 2010. Web. 11 Oct. 2017.

North Carolina Center on Actual Innocence. North Carolina's Innocence Projects, n.d. Web. 5 Oct. 2017.

Parascandola, Rocco, Graham Rayman, and Thomas Tracy. "Racist Maryland man who fatally stabbed black New Yorker admits his intent to kill African-American men." *Nydailynews.com.* New York Daily News, 23 Mar. 2017. Web. 3 Oct. 2017.

"Reining in Sanctuary Cities." Editorial. *The National Review.* The National Review, 29 Mar. 2017. Web. 3 Oct. 2017.

Resnick, Brian. "'They're not even people:' why Eric Trump's dehumanizing language matters." *Vox.com.* Vox Media, Inc., 7 Jun. 2017. Web. 11 Oct. 2017.

Stolberg, Sheryl Gay and Eric Lichtblau. "Sweeping Federal Review Could Affect Consent Decrees Nationwide." *Nytimes.com.* The New York Times, 3 Apr. 2017. Web. 7 Oct. 2017.

"The Cracked Podcast." Trump Country: What The Media Doesn't Want You To Know. *Earwolf.* Earwolf, 24 Oct. 2016. Web.

"The Intercept." Top Democrats Are Wrong: Trump Supporters Were More Motivated by Racism Than Economic Issues. Narr. Mehdi Hasan. *The Intercept.* The Intercept, 6 Apr. 2017. Web.

"The Nation's Immigration Laws: 1920 to Today." *Pew Research Center: Hispanic Trends.* Pew Research Center, 28 Sept. 2015. Web. 11 Oct. 2017.

United States. The White House. *Remarks by the President at the 50th Anniversary of the Selma to Montgomery Marches.* The White House, 7 Mar. 2015. Web. 7 Oct. 2017.

Weiner, Mark. "Syracuse's poverty rate remains among worst in nation, Census finds." *Syracuse.com.* The Post-Standard, 15 Sept. 2016. Web. 10 Oct. 2017.

Williams, Monica T. "The Link Between Racism and PTSD." *Psychology Today.* Psychology Today, 6 Sept. 2015. Web. 3 Oct. 2017.

Winsor, Morgan. "What to know about the case involving the Texas cop who shot a 15-year-old." *Abcnews.go.com.* ABC News, 3 May 2017. Web. 7 Oct. 2017.

About the Author

Dianne Liuzzi Hagan lives a multicultural life and writes about race, ethnicity, gender, politics, and cultural issues. She earned her MFA from Queens University of Charlotte in 2010 and an MS in Professional Education Studies with a concentration in multiculturalism from Le Moyne College in 2006. Her undergraduate degree is a dual BS in Speech Communication and English Education from Syracuse University. Her work has been published in *Interrace Magazine* and in the Greenhaven Press Current Controversies Anthology *Police Brutality*. She currently writes a serial-memoir blog titled *About Race*.
(http://aboutracewriter.blogspot.com)

Another Day in Post-Racial America

Another Day in Post-Racial America

Made in the USA
Middletown, DE
05 February 2021